Thinking Forward

OTHER BOOKS BY MICHAEL ALBERT

- *What Is To Be Undone*
- *Unorthodox Marxism* (with Robin Hahnel)
- *Marxism and Socialist Theory* (with Robin Hahnel)
- *Socialism Today and Tomorrow* (with Robin Hahnel)
- *Beyond Survival* (with Dave Dellinger)
- *Liberating Theory* (with Noam Chomsky, Lydia Sargent, Leslie Cagan, Robin Hahnel, Mel King, Holly Sklar)
- *The Quiet Revolution in Welfare Economics* (with Robin Hahnel)
- *The Political Economy of Participatory Economics* (with Robin Hahnel)
- *Looking Forward* (with Robin Hahnel)
- *Stop the Killing Train*

Thinking
Forward

Learning to

Conceptualize

Economic

Vision

Michael Albert

ARBEITER RING
Winnipeg, Manitoba

Arbeiter Ring Publishing
2-91 Albert Street
Winnipeg, Manitoba
Canada R3B 1G5

Copyright © 1997

Cover art and interior drawings by Tony Doyle.

Printed in Canada by the workers at Hignell Printing.

Canadian Cataloguing in Publication Data:

Albert, Michael, 1947–

Thinking forward, learning to conceptualize economic
vision

Includes bibliographical references.
ISBN 1-894037-00-6

1. Economics 2. Welfare economics. 3. Comparative economics. 4.
Distributive justice. 5. Industrial managment—employee participation. 6. Economic policy—Citizen participation. I. Title.

HB171.A422 1997   330   C97-920058-X

A man named Chi-liang tells this story to his ruler in an effort to dissuade him from his plans for war:

"I came across a man at Taihang Mountain, who was riding northwards. He told me he was going to the state of Chu."

"In that case, why are you headed north," I asked him.

"That's all right," he replied. "I have good horses."

"Your horses may be good, but you're taking the wrong direction."

"Well, I have plenty of money."

"You may have plenty of money, but this is the wrong direction."

"Well, I have an excellent charioteer."

"The better your horses," I told him, "the more money you have and the more skilled your charioteer, the further you will get from the state of Chu."

Contents

Preface

PARTLY, THIS BOOK IS ABOUT "PARTICIPATORY ECONOMICS," a goal for how to operate a humane economy. Arbeiter Ring Publishing seeks to implement the values and logic of participatory economics in the present. They have raised for themselves the same questions this book tackles, and they are trying in practice to provide working answers. That makes publishing with Arbeiter Ring very gratifying for me and, I hope, for the long list of authors they will attract in coming years. I thank them for creating a new radical publishing house in difficult times, and for developing a new participatory economic example in practice. I also thank them for publishing *Thinking Forward*. Nearly twenty years ago I helped found South End Press, which also seeks to actualize participatory economic values in practice. Later, I helped found *Z Magazine*, Left On Line, and most recently ShareWorld Systems. As a result, I know about the joys, frustrations, fear, and celebration associated with creating a new institution. Again, then, I am honored and pleased to have Arbeiter Ring publish *Thinking Forward*, particularly as their first title.

The chapters in this volume were initially presented in an online course in Left On Line's Learning On Line University and I would like to thank the students who took part in that experiment. The suggestions and insights they offered have in many instances been incorporated into this book.

Second, the ideas in *Thinking Forward* were developed with my longtime friend and writing partner, Robin Hahnel. We conceived the participatory economic model together and first wrote about it in detail in *Looking Forward* (South End Press, 1991) and *The Political Economy of Participatory Economics* (Princeton University Press, 1991). While the responsibility for this course in particular and also for the unorthodox approach of this book are mine, the intellectual content is joint, as are the words used in chapters 8 and 10.

Robin Hahnel has also taught a course in the Learning On Line University and has developed a book from the effort (South End Press, 1997). Those who complete this study of economic vision and who want to better understand the dynamics of contemporary economics are well advised to give it a close look.

Finally, in 1997 in the wake of endless mainstream hoopla about the victory of capitalism and markets and their inevitability and perfection, it is hard for most people to even entertain the idea of a different type of economy. To purchase a book on the subject is a welcome sign of commitment. I hope you persevere in conceiving, refining, and most importantly agitating for and winning a new economy and new society. I thank you in advance for your time and energies and I hope this book is worthy of them.

Introduction

Why have a book like this, anyway?

"[Capitalism] is not a success. It is not intelligent, it is not beautiful, it is not just, it is not virtuous—and it doesn't deliver the goods. In short, we dislike it, and we are beginning to despise it. But when we wonder what to put in its place, we are extremely perplexed."

—John Maynard Keynes

WHY VISION?

"[We seek] a condition of society in which there should be neither rich nor poor, neither master nor master's man, neither idle nor overworked, neither brain-sick brain workers, nor heartsick hand workers, in a word, in which all would be living in equality of condition and would manage their affairs unwastefully, and with the full consciousness that harm to one would mean harm to all—the realization at last of the meaning of the word commonwealth."

—William Morris

FOR SOME PEOPLE THE QUESTION "WHY VISION?" may appear silly. They feel that we obviously need vision to know where we are going. Vision tells us where we want to arrive and reveals how our present locale falls short of our desires. Vision raises hope and desire. It motivates and secures our efforts against temporary setbacks. How else can we organize our journey so it points in the right direction and so nothing about it diverts us from our destination? These are certainly reasonable reactions, yet others have serious doubts about pursuing vision.

"We can't know the future sufficiently to formulate vision sensibly," they argue. "To act as if you can is deceitful," they warn. And anyhow, "even if you could pose a sensible vision, it would be authoritarian to do so." To put icing on their argument, they inform us that: "The future must come from everyone's involvement and for a few people to pose a vision crowds out that involvement. If you start thinking about vision prematurely a few people will impose a future of their private design, rather than hosts of people collectively creating the future."

The critic's points are well taken and have been proposed by many folks, including, most notably, Noam Chomsky. Yet I am not convinced.

Can a critic of trying to develop economic vision really contest that to move forward wisely, we must know something about where we want to wind up? Surely social change strategies can't only react to what is, but must also seek what we want. History shows that well intentioned movements often failed even after defeating opponents because "in victory" they established new structures little better than the old ones. Wasn't this in part because most participants in these movements had nothing better clearly in mind? Can anyone really contest that to have compelling aims can help sustain struggle?

The critic, undaunted, replies that these are powerful arguments for vision, yes, but that they do not tell us how much vision and how detailed a vision we need, only that something is needed. Coming at the problem from the opposite direction the critic, such as Chomsky, will ask:

- Can anyone who advocates developing vision deny that history and society are so horribly complex that the future is largely beyond our predictive abilities?

- Can any visionary deny that to make believe one can predict future arrangements in detail is outrageous hubris?

• And can any advocate of developing a compelling vision deny that this can foster an egotistical attachment to one conception, reducing experiment, participation, and learning, and cramming history into an inflexible mapping that may have little or nothing to do with real human potentials? Surely this too has happened in history.

I agree that these "anti-visionary" correctives are important, but they don't tell us to do without vision, only not to get too detailed or regimented about what we propose.

So, in light of the good points raised on both sides of this debate, how should we approach vision generally and economic vision specifically? How much do we want? What attitude should we take toward what we adopt?

We seek a picture of a desired future sufficiently rich and detailed to provide hope and direction, but also respect careful analysis based on real knowledge. We understand our efforts to be cumulative, adaptable, and always the basis for more clarification, refinement, and improvement as we learn more through practice. We are not creating blueprints to confine ourselves, but disseminating the skills and knowledge needed for effectively conceptualizing and adapting vision. We recognize that people need and will use vision both for direction and for sustenance, and so we want to enlist and assist people in joining a collective, flexible, continually improving, visionary project of their own making.

The most effective opponents of too much vision, such as Chomsky, might still say that what we need is only to reduce hierarchy and injustice to an absolute minimum. It is enough that as we band into social movements to reduce hierarchy and injustice, we will learn more about how to accomplish our ends. To try to postulate anything more in the way of future vision now will narrow our view on the one hand, and likely be ill-conceived due to the complexity of the issues involved, on the other.

My reply, finally, is that critics of being visionary cannot have it both ways. If the world is so complex and the possibility for visionary error so great—which is all too true—then as with any other human endeavor, some care and thought is in order. And if there is no public effort at creating vision, employing publicly available tools and methods, then a relatively few folks with great intellectual confidence will take these tasks upon themselves privately. Such folks will be, by their training and their position in society, those who are conceptually well equipped to come up with ideas about new institutions and especially to voice them convincingly, but who are also, due to their élitist, academic biases, ill equipped for doing this humanely. In other words, by arguing against the need to publicly address issues of vision in sufficient detail, critics of vision ironically foster exactly the ends they wish to avoid: vision created by a self-defined élite, imposed on the many who are excluded from the creative process, and reflecting a narrow set of élite interests due to the authors' places in society.

To us, the real solution to the conundrum—that people seeking a better society need vision but that having vision can also do us harm—is not to reject vision in public while it is developed privately, but to debate visionary aims and goals publicly, and, more, to disseminate and clarify the methods by which vision is developed so that all people who wish to may partake of the project, confidently bringing to bear their own insights, interests, and experiences.

As to whether this approach can avoid the hubris of proposing too much, the élitism of trying to limit how many people participate in conceiving vision, or the sectarianism of trying to constrain future thought to narrow channels, history and practice will have to judge. But my unabashed aims in *Thinking Forward* are to develop clarity about values and methods of analysis and to elaborate concepts suited to describing and evaluating the defining institutions of a desirable economy. And to me this includes conceiving how production could be organized, the character of consumption, and what means of allocation would be employed, all sufficiently for assessment and refinement by others and for adaptation and use as a guide in developing programs for change. Anything less may be candy for the mind, but will have limited bearing on attaining a better world.

To begin to accomplish these ends as a preliminary step we have to know:

1. What is an economy—so that we know what we have to describe in order to have described an economic vision.

2. What aims we want an economy (that is, our economic

vision) to accomplish—so that we know what qualities we have to build into the economy we favor.

But before getting to these introductory issues, which are the main focus of our first chapter, there is one further matter to discuss.

READING THIS BOOK

"The disadvantage of exclusive attention to a group of abstractions, however well-founded, is that, by the nature of the case, you have abstracted from the remainder of things."

—Alfred North Whitehead

This book is compiled from a course on Conceptualizing Economic Vision given in the Left On Line (LOL) telecommunications system. The procedures for the course are typical for online courses generally. A lecture is posted. Students react and pose questions. Faculty and other students respond. Debate proceeds followed by another lecture at week's end. The course was successful and the idea for this book followed. To learn about LOL please use a web browser to visit *Z Magazine's* public site at www.lbbs.org.

The chapters in the book have three primary ends:

1. To understand the visionary economic model called participatory economics as well as the other contending visions called "market socialism" and "centrally planned socialism."

2. To teach how to judge these systems and especially to adapt them, or to conceive entirely different economic models.

3. To indicate how the social vision lessons of the course apply to other domains, for example conceptualizing gender, political, or cultural goals for modern societies.

In the chapters I try to be conversational and clear, but not simplistic. I start from scratch, assuming no prior knowledge of economics or social change struggle. This is not a textbook in the traditional sense, nor a history book, nor a survey of a field, nor a comprehensive rendition of my own views on economic vision, for that matter. It is, instead, very nearly an exact transcription of the lectures from an online course whose content was very much determined by its participants. It seeks to teach, to provoke, to elicit, much more than to create or to present.

As a means to these aims, each chapter includes a series of questions that are raised early in the chapter and only answered at the end. Settling on answers of your own before turning to the answers I offer will greatly increase the value of reading this book. Yes, you can just read *Thinking Forward* without trying to answer the questions yourself. But experience with this course in the Learning on Line University suggests that trying to puzzle out the many issues raised before reading my take on them will be far more instructive.

Let me put it even more bluntly: If I thought readers wouldn't think through the issues and try to answer the questions raised for themselves before reading my answers, I wouldn't bother publishing this volume.

1. Scene Setting

What is an economy and what aims might we have for an economy?

"Upon entering Paris which I had come to visit, I said to myself, here are a million human beings who would all die in a short time if provisions of every sort ceased to go towards this great metropolis. Imagination is baffled when it tries to appreciate the multiplicity of commodities which must enter tomorrow through the barriers in order to preserve the inhabitants from falling prey to all the convulsions of famine, rebellion, and pillage."

—Frederic Bastiat

"I wish that every human life might be pure transparent freedom."

—Simone de Beauvoir

WHAT IS AN ECONOMY?

HOW DO YOU ANSWER A QUESTION LIKE THIS? It initially seems so vague and broad to most folks that they are largely stymied. I suppose we could look the answer up somewhere, but the idea in these chapters is for each of us to create our own answers to all the many questions we raise, not to find and repeat someone else's, not least because existing answers may be wrong, or narrow, or even duplicitous. So, how about if we take it a step at a time?

First, what happens in an economy? Well, of course, people consume and produce things. So let's start with that:

> An economy is the set of institutions that facilitate and organize people producing and consuming things.

What then is *production*, what is *consumption*, what is an *institution*, and what does "facilitate and organize" mean?

Notice, we are already conceptualizing—that is, we are taking the world and finding within it aspects that we want to focus our attention on, then refining our understanding of these highlighted aspects by giving them names, in this case *economy*, *production*, *consumption*, and *institution*.

> The world is a huge interlocking web of "stuff." We pull from it components or facets that we want to highlight and to use as a basis for further analysis and understanding. These components we give names and they become concepts in our conceptual toolbox. Later, to create theory we explain our concepts' interrelations, to create vision we use our concepts to create new models, and to explain events we relate the events to the dynamics of our concepts. We choose particular facets of the world to become our basic concepts because we feel that using them at the core of our thinking will help us account for what is important without suffering more detail than we need.

PRODUCTION

When production happens something new emerges from stuff combined together. Think about a bicycle shop. The shop has inputs and outputs. The inputs are combined; the outputs result. The action in the middle is called work. The place where this happens is a workplace, such as Sally's Bike Repair Center.

• What are the inputs and outputs of production *processes*?

This is the first question we need to answer before next chapter. I'll get us started. In Sally's Bike Repair Center, surely bikes come out and rubber and steel go in, but what about Sally herself and her state of being? Or consider an auto plant. One thing that goes in is glass. One that comes out is a Chevrolet. But doesn't much more actually enter the plant and leave it? You might want to think about it for a few minutes before continuing. I hope you will answer in your own way, before you read my own answer at the end of this chapter. For now, however, let's just go on as if we already have the answer.

Knowing what the inputs and outputs of production are, how do we describe workplaces? They are institutions, you might say. Fine. But what is that? If "institution" is to be a concept we use in our thinking, as I indeed think it ought to be, what is the critical attribute that defines institutions and that distinguishes one from another?

This is arguably the hardest part of theorizing—reaching out into the familiar world and settling on basic concepts, including clarifying just what we mean by them in a way that helps us later, rather than narrowing our perceptions. Our concepts draw us toward some facets of reality, highlight some relations, attune us to seeing some features, but they also inevitably leave out other facets, obscure other relations, and turn us away from other features. If our concepts efficiently focus us on what matters for our investigative, analytic, or visionary purpose, they are good. But if they turn us away from what matters, or include so much that is peripheral that we can't ever get to the core of things, then they fail us. Settling on good concepts is a key step in doing any kind of intellectual work.

So, again, what is an institution? Is it the floor plan? Is it the size of the building or even the existence of a building? Is it the speed at which things happen? The quality of the results? These characteristics are often important for various concerns that one might have, but I think we can all agree they are not at the economic and social heart of the matter. But if they are not at the heart of what we want to focus on when we use the concept *institution*, what is?

Well, we know that there is something similar about, say, GM, Microsoft, and the local cannery that makes them all workplaces and that this is presumably what we want to get a grip on when addressing issues of work and production. It isn't their specific size, products, buildings, or locales. GM, Microsoft, and the local cannery have almost nothing in common on these axes. What they do have in common is instead something about the relations that exist, day in and day out, among the actors who get together in these institutions—something about their motivations, interests, behaviors, and choices. And this is what we implicitly have in mind, it seems to me, when we refer to an institution. We are not referring so much to material structures as to role structures. So let's just make this explicit. That is, to define our basic concept *institution* suppose we say that:

> An institution is a collection of social roles (plus, peripherally, some infrastructure and perhaps equipment, and the people who fill the roles). By social roles we mean things like union steward, mother, judge, manager, CEO, owner, worker.

But now, with this concept in our toolbox, we can easily see that the critical thing linking the businesses mentioned above is that they all embody the same basic defining role structures having to do with capitalists, workers, and managers, whose character we will investigate shortly.

More, in different economies it follows that we will have qualitatively different types of economic institutions, due to their having qualitatively different role structures. Feudalism has serfs and lords, capitalism has its own roles, and any new economic vision we come up with will have its own unique roles as well.

> In any economy, therefore, we have workplaces which have role structures by which production takes place via inputs and outputs. So if we are going to define an economic vision, part of the job will be defining these production institutions, and particularly their role structures.

So here are some more questions to consider as you proceed with this chapter. As usual, my own answers will appear at the end of the chapter.

- What are the primary roles within capitalist workplaces?
- Is a public school a workplace? What about a GM factory or a family? How about a church or school? Why or why not?

CONSUMPTION

Before taking up a new component of economics—consumption—note that we already have some ways to organize our thinking. We have defined one type of economic activity, which we have called production. We have said it has inputs and outputs (which you are supposed to be thinking about and we will get to in more detail soon), and have said that it is carried out in production institutions or workplaces, and that these have role structures (that you are also hopefully thinking about, and that we will also address further shortly). One important part of the art of doing theoretical, explanatory, or visionary work is to develop concepts and then build on them by adding new concepts only when they are really needed. There is no sense adding more things to remember unless they really help us. Before adding to our conceptual toolbox, therefore, we should always try to make do with what we already have. So what about consumption? Do we need some new concepts to handle it, or not?

We immediately recognize that consumption is another economic activity. It too has inputs and outputs that we can further conceptualize. It too is carried out in context of institutions which have role structures we can discern and describe. Since these few concepts go a long way, we already have some more questions to deal with as we proceed:

- What are the inputs and outputs of consumption activity?
- What distinguishes consumption activity from production activity?
- What are some consumption activity roles?
- Is a factory, a school, or a family a consumption institution? Why or why not?

See what comes to mind for these questions, if you have some time for it, and we will get to them shortly. And always try at first to answer using just the conceptual toolbox we are developing. If you can't, then by all means add more concepts until you can. But don't leap to answer from prior common sense or school knowledge. Try to answer only from the concepts we are developing. Appeal to your knowledge more broadly only as you must to augment what you can say within your new conceptual framework.

ALLOCATION

Now we turn to the sticky question of how production and consumption are facilitated and organized. What does this entail (in addition to another concept, *allocation*)?

Well, we know that there are a whole lot of people consuming and producing, and we know that there are a whole lot of places where all this activity goes on.

> Allocation is the name we give the institutions and processes that determine the inputs and outputs of the economy's activities and where they will wind up.

In each production institution, what is produced, how much, with what steps, by whom? And for each person and group of people, what is consumed, how much, and how is it gotten? Also, how does what is produced come to match what is sought for consumption and vice versa? How do outputs match up with inputs?

The answer to all these queries is that all this mixing and matching and determining is called allocation and is mediated by allocation institutions whose character may differ, of course, from economy to economy.

The market, for example, is an allocation institution. And so is central planning. And we might dream up some other allocation institutions as well, including say, decentralizing the economy into little separate self-sufficient units so that allocation is carried on entirely face to face by some type of barter. Each of these means of allocation—the market, central planning, and face to face barter—for example, are structural ways of determining who does what, where, in what quantities, for whom. They are institutions, which tells us that they embody particular roles that people must fill to benefit from the institution's offerings.

Once we think of markets as an institution, given our current conceptual toolbox, we know that we need to describe the associated role structure. Likewise, if we think of central planning this way, again, we have to describe the roles associated with central planning.

For markets, for example, we have buyers and sellers. There may be other refinements in a particular market economy, but we could go a long way toward seeing the defining features of markets if we revealed the institutionally determined motivations and behaviors of buyers and sellers and how their behaviors combine to influence allocation. For central planning we have order givers (planners) and order takers (workers) and about these roles we should also ask, supposing that we want to understand central planning, what motivations do they impose and what implications do they have? Indeed, for any economic vision, for comprehension we will need to:

> Describe the allocation institution in terms of the roles that it defines for economic actors and the ensuing dynamics and processes these roles promote and their implications for who does what, who gets what, and how people benefit or suffer in their economic lives.

In light of our new concept, allocation, some new questions arise for our consideration:

- In a market economy, what determines how much of the product each actor gets?
- And what determines, in a market economy, how much work each actor does?
- What is investment and what does it have to do with allocation?

So we are now at the point where we can somewhat clarify what we are trying to do.

> To define an economic vision, we need to define production, consumption, and allocation institutions that work successfully together and have qualities we like.

How do we know, however, what it is that we like? Suppose someone asked you what you think an economy ought to achieve to be a good economy. This is not so easy to answer. So, to proceed with defining an economic vision, we need to focus on some evaluative issues.

Evaluating Economies and Determining What We Want

"I would like to believe that people have an instinct for freedom, that they really want to control their own affairs. They don't want to be pushed around, ordered, oppressed, etc., and they want a chance to do things that make sense, like constructive work in a way they control, or maybe control together with others. I don't know any way to prove this. It's really a hope about what human beings are like, a hope that if social structures change sufficiently, those aspects of human nature will be realized."

—Noam Chomsky

Economies affect people. This is pretty obvious but nonetheless important to understand in more detail. Economies influence what we do (by providing roles we have to fill) and what we get from their productive output (by their allocation outcomes). These two facts in turn have much to do with our possible life stories. Are we doing interesting or boring things at work? Do we have power over our circumstances or are we bossed around by others? Do we starve, get by, or enjoy luxury? What happens to our personalities and potentials in the work that we do and the consuming we opt for?

> Evaluating an economy means asking how its institutions affect people. That is, what are the built-in implications for people's lives of the economy's production, consumption, and allocation institutions?

If the economy propels anti-social attitudes or distorts and under utilizes human capabilities or rewards people unjustly, these would be issues to take up in evaluating it. To make a judgment we must have some view of what is good and bad in the built-in dynamics of the economy so we have to broadly decide what we would like an economy to achieve. There are many possible answers:

1. We might want an economy to maximize output for our society. The economy that can produce the biggest pile of

stuff is the one we want, regardless of other effects.

2. We might want an economy to ensure that some set of people get the most possible return regardless of total output or what anyone else gets.

3. We might want an economy to yield identical outcomes for everyone, with the largest output consistent with that degree of equality.

I don't like any of these options, however, for pretty obvious reasons. The first could yield a gigantic pile of weapons or other stuff unsuited to human fulfillment and development. The second is élitist, enriching some at the cost of others. The third is mindlessly egalitarian since we all have different interests, tastes, and inclinations, so that this type of homogeneity is not an aim, but a nightmare.

I am going to instead propose some broad goals: equity, solidarity, diversity, and participatory self-management, plus efficiency, and, by implication, classlessness.

> *Equity* says we should have fair or just outcomes. No one should get more of a good thing or of a bad thing than he or she deserves.
>
> *Solidarity* means the economy should foster empathy among people and mutual respect and caring, rather than an attitude that you are my enemy or, in any event, that I don't care about your well-being.
>
> *Diversity* testifies to a belief that homogeneity is boring and we all benefit from diverse outcomes. Partly this is because it is a good hedge against errors. Partly it is because life is short and we can enjoy other people's different involvements vicariously.
>
> *Participatory self-management* means each person should be able to affect the decisions that in turn affect him or her in proportion as we are affected by those decisions. And, of course, the economic functions to produce, consume, and allocate in light of people's preferences and capacities and to attain these broader aims, should be carried out without waste (efficiency).

We could argue about these, I suppose, forever. My reasons for choosing these as the economic aims I want to see embodied in an economy probably stem from all manner of influences on my own thinking and values. But, I think among people concerned about social change, these broad goals should be pretty uncontroversial except that we might wonder if a system can address them all simultaneously, or if they are comprehensive enough to give us a system we will like.

My claims on behalf of these broad aims are very simple. In an economy, other things equal, if we have more of these attributes, it is better. If we have less, it is worse. More, these values together create comprehensive norms that can weed out bad and highlight good economic structures.

Classlessness, another value that we might espouse, is, for example, derivative of these aims because if you have classes rather than classlessness you are worse on all these values. Class division reduces equity, curtails solidarity, reduces diversity, limits self-management, and introduces various inefficiencies. So on the road to meeting the above criteria, you also strive toward classlessness.

But there is no need or reason to take my word that this is a good list of values for thinking about economic vision. One thing you might wish to do as we proceed is consider whether you think there may be some desirable value you would like to see implemented in a good economy that will be left out if we take just my favorites as our guide. Or, for that matter, you might want to question the desirability of any of my five, listed above.

Again, my own personal justification for these five values is that they seem to me to be consistent with and necessary for a maximum of personal fulfillment and development for each individual and for the whole population as a collective, consistent with the idea that everyone should have as good a shot at fulfillment and development as anyone else. Also, they are especially suitable for methodically evaluating the components of an economy. These are therefore going to be the values that guide my choices during the following chapters, but if you wish to take into account other values as well, please do so as you proceed. The same methodology I will be using with my favored values should prove apt for you with yours, in any event. And so here is another question to ponder:

- What do you think of this discussion of values and economics, and what alternative suggestions might you have for the value system we utilize in our work to come?

Answers to Questions

"... the validity of a particular theory is a matter of its logical derivation from the general assumptions which it makes. But its applicability to a given situation depends upon the extent to which its concepts actually reflect the forces operating in that situation."

—Lionel Robbins

A word, first, about the point of these questions. The really important things overall in these exercises are:

1. To think about economic concepts and vision methodically and comprehensively. The usual approach is, instead, to apply some experiences, or lessons, or beliefs, or a little thought, and race to conclusions. This is often OK in life—often, indeed, there is no time for more. But when trying to theorize some domain (such as economics) or design some system (such as an economy) far more care and discipline is needed.

2. To actually believe in our own thoughts and draw conclusions from them. I mean this seriously. The vast majority of folks would, I think, arrive at views quite disdainful of existing structures, were they to do these exercises in a non-threatening context. But, having done this, it would then have few if any implications for many people's attitudes toward the structures addressed or the actual economy we live in. Some kind of weight of experience, or history, or pessimism, or whatever, would override their reasoned assessments. Instead, we should develop concepts and aims, apply the concepts to understand situations and processes in light of aims, reject what fails, and support what seems worthy. We have to be flexible and humble about our judgments, of course. But I don't see much value in arriving at views, and then dispensing with them in conversations with friends and in our estimates of our role in society.

So what about the questions asked this chapter? Taking the content of the chapter so far as a starting point, and in light of our purposes, the following brief answers would be more than satisfactory, to my thinking.

• What are the inputs, and what are the outputs of production processes?

Inputs include material items (such as resources, goods produced elsewhere, and infrastructure), but also people's work or labor, people themselves (including the level of knowledge they have, their health, the moods and levels of fulfillment they have, and their personalities and skills), and the social relations of the workplace (including the roles of the workplace and the rules of its operation, and relations between actors). Saying these are all inputs means that all these entities enter into the production process as aspects needed for it to occur and influencing its outcomes, and that they are reproduced, altered, or used up in the process.

As obvious as every aspect of the above answer is once we see the items listed, many people indicating inputs stop with material things plus people's work. And despite the fact that "material things plus work" is also the answer most often offered by mainstream economists and even most schools of radical economists, this is woefully inadequate. Imagine a psychologist listing human interests and leaving out sex, or a nutritionist listing inputs to the body and leaving out water. Similarly, what sense does it make to list economic inputs and leave out people's skills, knowledge, and emotions?

Well, in fact, the strange truth is that for some purposes this can make good sense. Remember, we choose concepts to highlight features that we care about and that we need to pay attention to for our subsequent thinking and visualizing to be effective. But what if your priority was only to maximize profits for an owner, regardless of effects on anyone else save insofar as these effects mattered for the size of profits? Then for you to use concepts that left out certain features that we as citizens or workers might think are important to include, given our different priorities, may make sense. This is why, for accountants paid by owners of companies, the "bottom line" does not include any reference whatever to the effect of economic life on producers and consumers, but only includes reference to monetary costs and revenues and, ultimately, profits. The theorist has an agenda, and what matters to that agenda is conceptualized, while what doesn't matter to it, or what might distract from it, is avoided.

In any event, to continue with the answer to the question, outputs of production processes certainly include material products and by-products of the production process and services produced, but they also include people (with potentially changed knowledge, health, moods, fulfillment levels, personalities, and skills) and social relations (which, likewise, may be altered due to the production process). Here too the absence of the latter two categories of output from production typifies most economists' views and, obviously, once the point is made, consigns them to inadequacy—at least regarding our priorities. For how could you possibly evaluate a production institution vis-à-vis its effects on solidarity, equity, diversity, and self-management, if you don't even include in the conceptual toolbox you use reference to effects on human personality, knowledge, skills, and social relations?

How could it make any sense to list the inputs and outputs of work and not list the state of being of the people who participate in it and the state of social relations among them if one is concerned with designing (or evaluating) economic models to benefit people? How can you design the model to benefit factor x, when you leave factor x out of the conceptual apparatus you use in building your model in the first place? You can't, obviously.

On the other hand, however, to repeat a critical point for understanding the logic of conceptual systems, if your focus is not people per se, but profit or material surplus, and if you care about people only as far as you must to address those other profit or power centered aims, then different criteria guide what parts of reality you decide to highlight. That is, with profits as your priority it makes sense, however inhumane it may be, to use concepts that leave effects on people out of the analytic picture save to the degree that the effects bear on profits.

I want to elaborate (you may feel "beat to death" would be a better term for what I am doing) this point about concepts just a bit further before proceeding to the next question. We are trying to build a theory. We want concepts that highlight what we care about, and anything that significantly affects what we care about. Someone might say that air goes in the windows of the workplace or that dirt goes into the workplace congealed to the incoming raw materials. But obviously these are not features we need to put in our theory at the level of basic concepts. Instead, what is it that we do care about in a workplace?

Each worker has a certain physical condition going in, and perhaps another, even including a lost limb, say, or just plain exhaustion, coming out. Notice, if we simply elide this from our theory, then the recognition leaves our thoughts as well. This is precisely what happens in what is called neoclassical economics, or professional economics, a framework that highlights some facets and ignores others according to a criteria that distorts understanding in the interests of élites and ignores the plight of workers.

• What are the primary roles within capitalist workplaces?

Well, there are those who own the place and by virtue of this have a claim on profits and have ultimate authority over operations. They may have inherited their deed to ownership, they may have begun the firm themselves and worked fantastically hard making it successful, or they may have bought the place. Regardless, we call these folks capitalists.

Then there are those who have considerable control over their own circumstances of work and usually also over the definition of work of many other people as well. They have their position as manager, engineer, lawyer, or doctor, etc., by virtue of educational certification and monopolized skills, knowledge, and access to information and decision-making authority. I call these folks coordinators.

And then there are people who have nearly no control over their own conditions of work, or over anyone else's either, and whose circumstances are determined only by their ability to win higher wages or better conditions through organization with others in like straits. These are the workers.

Of course, we could refine endlessly beyond this, but these three classes are, I think, a sufficient demarcation for most broad analytic and visionary purposes. With contrary interests to one another and different world views arising from the different roles they fulfill in the economy, these three classes contend over quality of circumstance and share of productive output, as well as for power over outcomes. They even have different agendas for what an economy should be, a point we have already touched on in explaining why mainstream economic theory leaves out some focuses that we find critical.

• Is a public school a workplace; what about a GM factory, a family? Why or why not?

If we define a workplace as a place where inputs are transformed into outputs, then, yes, of course, all these are workplaces. If we confine the term workplace to refer to places where production in this broad sense occurs and where it is also the primary defining feature of the institution, then no, the school and family are not workplaces. It is a matter of the conceptual breadth that we want our choice of words to have at any given time. And since such institutions must partake of economic involvement to get their inputs and provide their outputs, I think it makes sense to pay attention to them as workplaces to precisely that extent.

• What are the inputs and outputs of consumption activity?

Consumption and production are each economic activity, distinguishable only by the fact that in the former the focus is on the items taken in (and the level of human fulfillment immediately resulting) whereas in the latter the focus is on the items (material or service) made available as outputs. But the answer for inputs and outputs to production does quite nicely for inputs and outputs of consumption as well, with only a few minor word changes. In and out of each we have material things (some natural and some produced, some sought, and some as by-products), and people including their mood, fulfillment, and attributes (changing, perhaps, along the way), and social relations (again, subject to change).

• What distinguishes consumption activity from production activity?

Only the focus of attention of the person doing the labeling.

• What are some consumption activity roles?

When we consider activity by roles, there is some difference between consumption and production because of the institutions in which most of what we will generally want to call production or consumption takes place. Consumption, as we will most often use the word, occurs via choices made in some living unit or group of such units. Thus, in different societies with different organization of living units, there may be quite different attitudes about consumption and different rules by which it is carried out. Does a patriarch make all choices, or parents, or a tribal elder? Are there taboos and requirements? Do people meet and discuss options? Do children have a say? And of course, it is also relevant to consider the degree to which class allegiance alters one's consumption role by affecting one's attitudes and options.

• Is a factory, a school, or a family a consumption institution? Why or why not?

Clearly, yes, if we view them in terms of what they take in, or in terms of their place in the economy as recipients of outputs from elsewhere, which is exactly how we ought to view them when we are thinking about the consumption part of economic activity. However, when we have on other hats, these institutions rightfully take on other primary aspects.

- In a market economy, what determines how much product each actor gets?

Monopolization, unionization, consciousness and organization, prior distribution of wealth and assets, race, gender, age, laws, government intervention, supply and demand, and so on. In short, bargaining power.

For example, suppose you produce some needed product and corner the market—that is, you become a monopoly or monopsony. You now have more power than if there were many other firms offering the product. You can extract more payment. Or imagine you are a small business and I am a very big client of yours—you depend on me to exist and I could go elsewhere. Then you have another small client who can't go elsewhere to get your service or product, and who depends on you. I have great relative power in our transaction. But you have great relative power in the transaction with the smaller client.

Suppose I am a worker. Whether I am in a union or not changes my bargaining power. Suppose I am a woman or Latino worker in a sexist or racist context or in a society in which these oppressive dynamics are absent—my bargaining power changes accordingly.

The point is, in a market economy buyers and sellers do not, as the usual rhetoric informs us, transact business with prices and the character of the exchange globally set regardless of their individual relations. Instead, prices for the same good and services for the same payment often vary dramatically depending on the relative bargaining power of the buyers and sellers. If people living in a poor community cannot travel far, then a local supermarket may be able to charge them more for carrots than the same supermarket would be able to charge rich people in a different neighborhood, able to shop elsewhere.

- And what determines, in a market economy, how much work each actor does?

Again, power, and the wills of the actors who have that power.

- What is investment and what does it have to do with allocation?

Investment is just a decision to apply certain resources, energies, and materials to creating new productive facilities, relations, and capacities to be utilized in the future. It is important by virtue of influencing the playing field tomorrow and thereafter. The relation of investment to allocation is that some amount of society's product is earmarked, during the allocation process, for investment rather than for meeting immediate ends. Investment is not intrinsically bad and has no implication regarding who gets what or the goals of innovations. Investment in a particular type of economy, however, will be contoured by that economy's norms to have certain qualities, which we may or may not like.

- What do you think of this discussion of values and economics, and what alternative suggestions might you have for the value system we utilize in our work to come?

The best way for me to answer this question will be to proceed with chapter 2.

2. Existing Visionary Options

What kind of economic goals have been espoused, and what are their virtues and faults?

"People's lives are in turmoil. There is a sense of crisis for men as well as for women, and for children too. Do we have an idea or even a glimmering about how people can and should live, not as victims as in the past for women, nor as atoms just whirling around on their own trajectories, but as members of a human community and as moral agents in that community?"

—Barbara Ehrenreich

This chapter focuses on various existing economic options and evaluates their production, consumption, and allocation role structures in light of the values enunciated in chapter 1.

Further Discussion of Values and Economies

"'Incapacity of the masses.' What a tool for all exploiters and dominators, past present and future, and especially for the modern aspiring enslavers, whatever their insignia ... Nazism, Bolshevism, Fascism, or Communism. 'Incapacity of the masses.' This is a point on which reactionaries of all colors are in perfect agreement ... and this agreement is exceedingly significant."

—Voline

As noted last chapter, economies influence what we do (by providing roles that we have to fill) and what we get from the productive output (by affecting allocation outcomes). These two facts in turn have much to do with our possible life stories.

If the economy propels anti-social attitudes or distorts and under-utilizes human capabilities, or if it rewards people unjustly or creates hostilities among people, or if it wastes time and effort needlessly or inexorably distorts personalities or violates the ecology, these would be issues to take up in evaluating it. The evaluative task is therefore to assess the built-in dynamics of any economy and their inevitable implications for people's lives.

So what would we like an economy to achieve in the way of broad general aims for people's lives? I noted last chapter five values meant to be necessary and (at the broad level) sufficient as evaluative norms for designing and judging economies. Now let's develop each a bit further.

First, *equity* says that we should have fair or just outcomes. No one should get more of a good thing or a bad thing than he or she deserves.

The idea isn't, however, to have a fair playing field and then a kind of land grab in which everyone starts at the same time with no advantages. In such contests outcomes can and generally are still unequal even if we go so far as to handicap fast runners with extra weight— that's why people in land grabs run like maniacs, because some get good land and some bad.

Our aim isn't, therefore, to have a fair contest leading to gross disparity of outcomes. Our aim is to attain fair outcomes. And so the question arises, what are fair outcomes? In talking about material distribution and about life circumstances, what should be our criteria for what people get? And so here is our first thought question for this chapter, to be answered before undertaking chapter 3:

- Beyond some vague notion of equity, what should be the actual criteria of remuneration and disposition of economic responsibilities?

How do we determine how much people are paid, that is, what share of output they receive?

Second, *solidarity* means the economy should foster empathy, mutual respect, and caring among people, rather than an attitude that you are my enemy or, in any event, I don't care about your well-being.

This value requires little explanation, I think. If economic functions and requirements produce sociality and solidarity, good. If they produce hostility and anti-social attitudes, bad. It would seem that only a psychopath would contest this.

Third, *diversity* merely testifies to a belief that homogeneity is boring and we all benefit from diverse outcomes.

Diversity of outcomes is a good hedge against errors. If everything is always done one way, then if that one way is wrong one has to start over from scratch. But if there are generally many approaches employed simultaneously, then when one proves detrimental there are others to choose among, well conceived and tested.

Also, diversity is valuable because life is short and we can enjoy other people's different involvements vicariously or via their product. We get pleasure, that is, appreciating the products and attainments and life stories of others who choose different pursuits than ours. We need to put diversity in our brief list, as compared to many other values we might mention, because otherwise one could attain the other aims we have enumerated by simply homogenizing everything into exact oneness. Diversity is not redundant, therefore, but essential to the list.

Fourth, *participatory self-management* means that each person should have a fair say over his or her own life.

But what is a fair say? Well, we should be able to affect the decisions that in turn affect us, and we should be able to do it in proportion as we are in turn affected. But please notice—this is not just one person, one vote nor is it consensus decision-making, nor any other singular accounting approach, for that matter. One person, one vote is sometimes useful, sometimes not, because it gives identical impact on outcomes to each person, not proportionate impact. Likewise, consensus is also sometimes useful, sometimes not, because it ultimately gives veto power to each participant.

Clearly there is no point, pragmatic or ethical, in the person on the other side of the plant having the same say as I do over how I arrange my desk space. To give others that power over my space is not democracy in action, but a kind of knee-jerk notion of democracy leading to waste, bedlam, or fisticuffs. Participatory self-management instead allots to each actor a say in decisions proportionate to the degree he or she is affected by the decisions. This seems to be what most people really mean by democracy when considering their own lives and to be what we ought to mean by it, in any event. My desk or work area is, save for implications it may have on others, my concern and no one else's.

> Fifth, an economy must also fulfill economic aims: that is, it has to deliver the products desired and it has to do this without wasting anything that people care about (which is called being *efficient*).

So what is efficiency? This is not so obvious, I think, and therefore bears a bit more comment. In the abstract, there is no such thing as efficiency per se. There is only efficiency in light of some agreed aims and valuations.

Efficiency means using "assets" fully, effectively, and without waste. If you have waste, then you could attain whatever positive ends you got without the waste and therefore with improvement. So anyone sane wants to be efficient in this technical sense of avoiding waste.

But please notice, if we say that the end sought is maximizing profits and we place no value on the well-being of the work force, then not utilizing every last ounce of energy, even if doing so means disempowering workers entirely, is inefficient. On the other hand, if we value worker well-being so that we see it as an asset that we care about or even part of our goal, then we get a very different view of what is efficient and what isn't.

In today's society the word efficient is taken to mean not wasteful, but also correct, mature, professional, careful, reasoned, and so on, and is therefore deemed good. But it is also taken to mean getting the most profit from available inputs regardless of the impact on anyone or anything outside the transaction. And this is not good and therein arises the source of confusion.

In any event, to return to our list of values, my claims about these evaluative criteria are intuitively pretty obvious but hard to demonstrate logically.

1. In an economy, other things equal, if we have more of these attributes, the economy is better. If we have less, it is worse.

2. If we attain these five aims to a great degree, we will also attain or be in a position to attain virtually any other desirable economic value anyone could propose.

The list of broad aims is useful, therefore, in being both necessary and sufficient to our overall goals. Economies often demarcate people into groups with opposed interests such that people in one such group are better off and have more power than people in others. These economically defined groups are called classes, and classlessness, for example, is an aim that emerges naturally from those we have chosen because if you have classes, as compared to not having them, you are worse on all these values. Class division reduces equity (the dominant class has more than its subordinates), curtails solidarity (classes struggle with one another), reduces diversity (within classes homogeneity is the rule), and limits self-management (as one class has preponderant power over others). The elimination of classes improves all these criteria. So, with our values as guide, clearly no classes is better than classes.

What about ecology? How come we don't have a separate value for, say, sustainability? Certainly lots of progressive economists do list such a value and of course we in fact have such values ourselves. So why not list it? Is it really implicit in the values we do list?

I will first tell you the actual history. When we first developed the participatory economic model, Robin Hahnel and I thought about these valuative issues pretty much as you are doing in these exercises, though over a longer time, of course. And when we thought about values to organize our structures around, the aims that roles we would advocate would try to attain, we came up with the values I offered here and nothing about ecology. I have to admit, with some embarrassment, that this wasn't because we consciously assessed the possibility of including an ecological value and decided not to. The truth is, it just wasn't on our minds.

Now the interesting thing is, I think, it didn't matter that we were not as attentive as we ought to have been to this issue. That is, I honestly think the economy that emerges from applying the values listed so far is just as good regarding ecology as it would have been had we put in another value highlighting the ecology. I'll go even further. I think it is better regarding ecology than what many Greens advocate for the economy, starting from sustainability as their primary aim.

Why do I say these things? Well, the values we have enumerated will cause us to require of our economic institutions that they account for ecological effects insofar as these impact on human well-being and development. The values we have chosen will not, however, cause us to design our economic institutions to have built-in features for judging the ecology, or nature, or particular species, regardless of implications for people. And I happen to think that this makes good economic sense. If a society wants to impose on its economy that regardless of economic impact on people a particular species must be defended, that is fine. And the economy ought to be able to accommodate such extra-economic (in this case ecological) requirements. But the economy itself should not do this a priori. The economy—in my view, at least—ought to provide people the means to determine their economic actions in accord with their desires and capacities and in tune with others doing likewise, but without prejudging issues that are extra-economic.

Some Greens, as another example, argue that scale of operations, or degree of industry, are critical matters that must be dealt with in principle at the level of guiding values. They will argue, that is, that a good economy is one that always and aggressively (or even maximally) promotes small scale, or that employs industry only as a last resort. I think, instead, that such aims, as a matter of principle, make no sense at all, economically or ecologically. What an economy ought to do is settle on scale of operations for firms, or on levels and types of technologies, all in accord with higher values, such as, in our case, equity, self-management, and so on. Sometimes a larger scale will make sense for a project or workplace. Sometimes new technologies ought to be used. The idea is that the economy should provide actors the information needed to make these judgments, rather than making the judgments automatically due to some built-in abstract norm.

Still, at each step in these chapters, if you feel strongly that sustainability, or any other value, should be considered, please do so. At all points, please consider whether what I am saying is missing something or not, and by all means please incorporate whatever additional features, or change whatever features I offer, as you see fit for developing your own economic vision.

To summarize, I think the models we develop using the values enunciated here will be attuned to ecological valuations and choices precisely as far as these impact on human well-being and development—and will also be able to honor constraints imposed by ecological choices that might be made on other grounds, for example, the rights of other species. Our economic vision will, of course, attend to sustainability, since to have an economy that isn't sustainable is catastrophic from the human point of view.

So, for now anyway, and with the caveat that you should do otherwise if you see fit, we can plausibly take our goals as the five noted. Could we choose other combinations of values that might also be as necessary and as sufficient? Yes, I think perhaps we could. These few are chosen, I would say, in the belief that they are well suited to guiding economic evaluation and design. I think they will make our job easier than most other ways of highlighting things and so until the experience of using them proves otherwise, I proceed. Indeed, this is always how we choose concepts, methods, and values for our toolbox. We want to include what is useful to attaining our intellectual and practical aims and we want to leave out what would waste our time or distract or distort our efforts. Too little detail or any wrong detail is no good. But so is too much detail.

EXISTING ECONOMIC MODELS

"Few markets can ever have been as competitive as those that flourished in Britain in the first half of the nineteenth century, when infants became deformed as they toiled their way to an early death in the pits and mills of the Black Country. And there is no lack of examples today to confirm the fact also that well functioning markets have no innate tendency to promote excellence in any form. They offer no resistance to forces making for a descent into cultural barbarity or moral depravity."

—Robert Solo

Suppose someone asked how many different stereo systems are there to choose from. You might make a list of the major components (suppose it is amplifier, receiver, speakers) and then count the instances in each group. If there were 8 types of amp, and 5 types of receiver, and 12 types of speaker (not just different colors, but really different types), and if you could mix and match these in any combination, then there would be 8x5x12 = 480 different unique types of stereo system to choose from. If some components were incompatible with others, however, the total would drop, perhaps quite a bit.

Now consider economies. How many distinct economic models are there to choose from? Well we can usefully think of economies as including ownership relations, production institutions, and allocation institutions. If we list the types available for each of these components, and check for compatibility problems, we can enumerate all existing (and perhaps all possible) types of economic models that we might choose from for our future.

Why did I leave out consumption institutions, and put in ownership relations? Well, because variations in the former prove in practice not to be so critical to the overall character of modern economies that we might consider in thinking about an economic vision, and therefore not so important for us to highlight in this book, whereas variations in the latter, ownership relations, do prove to be a particularly critical factor in determining the defining character of economies.

So, what possible choices for institutions do we have?

- Briefly, for ownership relations, any economy can have private ownership, state or public ownership, or collective ownership, and that's it. That's the whole menu of ownership options we have to choose from: four options.

- For production relations, our visionary economy can have hierarchical workplace structure, formal but unimplimented workers' control, or participatory council structure. And that's it. Three options, broadly speaking, are all I know of. (Of course each can have many sub-variants, but that is a different issue.)

- And finally, for allocation relations, our visionary economy can have markets, central planning, or a combination of the two, complete decentralization, or participatory planning. And, ignoring sub-variants, again, that's it. Four options.

So to figure out all possible economies, we can just ask how many combinations there are, remembering that combinations which can't hold together because of incompatibilities have to be ruled out. The total number of unique combinations is 3x3x4 = 36. But it turns out that once we evaluate each of these individually things simplify dramatically, because many combinations just don't work together.

1. We can choose variants on capitalism—which have private ownership, hierarchical production relations, and markets with more or less government (central) intervention.

2. Or we can choose variants on (what I call) coordinatorism (usually misleadingly called "socialism")—which have collective or state ownership, hierarchical production relations or formal but unimplemented workers' control, and more or less markets or central planning.

3. Or we can choose variants on a system we might call decentralized community economics—which can have any compatible combination of the ownership and organizational features, but is always organized into in a myriad of small locales each of which functions autonomously from the rest, self-sufficiently, and without allocation relations among them.

4. Or we can choose variants on participatory economics—which has proportionate collectively organized ownership, nested democratic council structures, and participatory planning.

To get more models, someone has to come up with other types of institutions or show that some other combinations of the ones we have already named are viable. This is not necessarily an impossible task, to be sure. Indeed, this book purports to provide the kind of conceptual approach needed to do it well. (Of course, in a real society, economies don't exist in the abstract, as models, but only in combination with states, kinship spheres, cultures, and so on.)

And thus arise a few questions to consider before moving on to chapter 3:

• We have deduced the possibility of 3x3x4 = 36 different conceivable economic systems including unique combinations of the components. How come we are able to boil this down to only four broad economic types? And why aren't there more than thirty-six that are conceivable? Or, can you conceive of more?

- Who advocates these different models, and why?
- What are the class relations of each of the four models and how do they arise from the basic institutions employed?

JUDGMENTS

"Woe betide those who seek to save themselves the pain of mental building by inhabiting dead men's minds."

—G.D.H. Cole

If we have confidence in our conceptual toolbox, to render judgments on these models is not so difficult as it might at first seem. We need only assess their basic institutions using the evaluative standards we decided to highlight—equity, solidarity, diversity, self-management, and associated efficiency. If we are going to be disciplined about this, as we ought to be, then if we find that a basic component institution is bad on one or more of these counts, we should want to reject it from our preferred economic vision. This is no different from deciding that amplifiers that use tubes are too costly, or receivers without FM are too inflexible, or that speakers that don't generate enough volume are insubstantial, and ruling these out on such grounds while moving on to compose a preferred stereo system from the remaining possible components. The logic for economies is essentially the same. Rule out economic components that violate our aims. Build a workable, desirable economy out of those components that further our aims by mixing and matching them into a workable whole system. Nothing subtle is at work here. We consider component ownership options, production relations options, allocation options, and then we have the basis for thinking about economies as a whole.

OWNERSHIP OPTIONS

First, consider private ownership. We know, and I am not going to rehearse all the evidence and arguments for want of time, that private ownership means that capitalists almost exclusively monopolize wealth. This is contrary to equity (no matter what precise definition we ultimately give it), and to solidarity (haves and have-nots will not be getting along well), and to self-management (haves will have more say than have-nots), and so we simply have to rule it out as a possible component of our economic vision.

Another way of saying it would be to say that we immediately reject private ownership on the grounds that rather than producing classlessness, it produces class division (with capitalists on top), because class divisions are incompatible with attaining our four evaluative norms. I know that people spend lifetimes discussing this, as if there is something complicated involved. But there isn't. And since you are reading a book on conceptualizing economic vision, I will assume you already know this and not waste a whole lot of time on the tangential issues, however much fun we might have rehearsing them.

Next, consider state or public ownership. Well, we know that under this option the state has ultimate control over productive property, either directly or as representative of the public. And even though the state tells us they will look out for the whole population's interest, we know that:

1. Even if the state did look out solely for the public welfare and even if its caste of bureaucrats were rapidly rotated and accountable, state management of economic affairs would still not be self-management but management from the top down.

2. If you set aside some group to have major powers they will likely develop the means to institutionalize themselves and then use their power for their own benefit at the cost of society, as in the history of Stalinism, for example. Thus there is no equity either.

So it follows that to be true to our values we must reject state or public ownership for our economic goal on grounds that intrinsic authoritarianism thwarts self-management and also equity. You may now be thinking to yourself, hey, this is too quick, too cavalier, too simple. But is it? Really?

Go back to the example of the stereo. If we establish some norms, for example we say that our system has to be able to hit some notes, or volume, or whatever, and we assess a possible component and by its very structure and definition it cannot do what we want, it seems to me if we are serious about the norms we established, we must reject the component. Surely if this applies for stereos, it also applies for economies—more so, if anything, since so much more is at stake.

Next, we can consider collective ownership. First, it refers to a situation in which everyone equally owns every productive unit—though not peoples' clothes or houses, for example. This sounds good, but what does mean?

If it means that everyone has an equal say in the disposition and control of each institution, that would clash with participatory self-management as we have defined it and thus we would have to reject it. In practice, however, this formulation of equal say for all in all matters is a bit hard to envision in any event.

If it means no one has any say or any claims by virtue of ownership because ownership is equalized, then this ownership option is essentially neutral, or absent, with no decision making or distribution implications at all, thus leaving the economy's fate to be decided by other features. So we could certainly employ it, with no fanfare but also with no loss. It would have no implications for any of the values we are pursuing or for anything else, for that matter. (Perhaps we should break collective ownership into the two options, equal say and no implications for say, but for convenience I am only going to treat the second, neutral version. If you would like to address the other version, by all means go ahead.)

So, what have we discovered about ownership? We don't like private or state ownership. We can abide collective ownership in its neutral sense (though not with any glee as it has neither good nor bad implications).

PRODUCTION RELATIONS OPTIONS

First, how about hierarchical workplace structure? Well, what is it? The idea is simple enough. There is a hierarchy of status, power, and reward associated with jobs, and people fit at different levels depending on the job they get. Think of a job as a collection of tasks and responsibilities. Different tasks and responsibilities (take out the trash, deliver the mail, talk to clients, take orders, put this ratchet in that slot, design the product, solve personnel problems, make policy decisions, or whatever) embody different skill and knowledge prerequisites and cause the person involved to have to do different things, with different effects on the person including different implications for the person's status, power, and reward.

Now for there to be a hierarchy, it is both necessary and sufficient that jobs be defined by combining like quality tasks and responsibilities with one another into relatively homogenous packages. Thus we get janitors, secretaries, line workers, managers, engineers, and so on, with jobs that are differentially empowering and differentially rewarding in circumstances and also remuneration. How do we evaluate this option, familiar in nearly every production institution in advanced capitalist societies and the old Soviet Union and every other contemporary economy as well?

Well, we can see right off that this option offers only homogenized jobs (and therefore not much diversity), authoritative decision making from the top (by those with more empowering work assignments and circumstances), more fulfilling conditions and more reward for some actors than others (depending on which quality job you get), and a situation with those below hostile to those above and vice versa. The option scores rather poorly, that is, on all our axes of evaluation.

Sometimes folks have doubts about the claim that class division actually reduces diversity. After all, aren't multiple anything more diverse than one of the same thing, and if so, isn't having three or four classes bound to be more diverse, whatever its other failings, than having classlessness? Well once we have classes we have large sectors of people with shared interests, arrayed in a hierarchy of reward and power. A significant part of the existence of each class becomes defending its niche, so to speak. This means there are powerful pressures causing all members of the class to adopt certain postures. With classlessness such forces are absent and what we are owes more to our own initiative and preference.

Is this real, or just rhetoric? Consider music, sports, entertainment of other sorts, reading material, eating habits, daily life habits, and so on. Are there large commonalities within classes, and big differences from class to class? Can we as a result with some reasonable accuracy predict people's tastes and preferences, values and views, in diverse domains of life, merely knowing their class affiliation? Can we guess a people's class if we know they listen to country music? Or if they prefer classical? What if they read the *New York Times* as opposed to a supermarket tabloid? Of course, other factors influence these choices, too, including markets, but class on its own seems to me to have this impact—it constrains and delimits the options of people in ways that limit and homogenize outcomes. And, as a result, it stems diversity.

In any event, even without a lot of detailed analysis (which is very worthwhile if you have the time for it) we can immediately reject hierarchical workplace structure as not fit for our economic vision since it fosters class stratification—workers at the bottom and then coordinators, or then coordinators and capitalists depending on the type of economy—which is inconsistent with equity, self-management, solidarity, and even diversity.

The second option for production relations is what is called above formal but unimplemented workers' control. The thing I have in mind here is a system that has in fact existed, for example in the former Yugoslavia. In each workplace there is a council of all the workers which has full authority over all decisions. The workers, organized into councils, have ultimate authority. However, we also know that that these councils choose, for reasons we'll understand after talking about allocation, to have homogenized jobs and to hire managers and plant bosses to rule over work, so that the actual result is a hierarchical workplace structure.

Therefore, despite its formal merits—workers' power is at least formally recognized—we reject formal but unimplemented workers' control for the same reason as we reject hierarchical workplace structure, because in practice it is a coordinator ruled workplace obstructing the values we favor. The origin of the hierarchy is not an imposition from the defined production relations, but an imposition from the allocation system on each workplace. Nonetheless in Yugoslavia with formal but unimplemented workers' control, the structure of roles in each workplace was only marginally distinguishable in practice from those in a U.S. Ford or a Soviet Lada factory.

So what about balanced job complexes? We will of course spend considerable time on this option later. For now, briefly, the idea is that we combine tasks and responsibilities into jobs so that each job is comparable to all others for quality of work experience, status, and particularly for empowerment implications even though each has its own particular combination of features. And, likewise, we incorporate an array of workplace councils to facilitate participatory proportionate decision making. Balanced job complexes mean that:

1. Every individual regularly does both conception and execution in a balanced combination so that she or he is prepared to participate effectively in decision-making;

2. No individual long occupies positions that present unu-

sual opportunities to monopolize influence, knowledge, or skills relevant to general decision-making; and

3. There is an equal distribution of the costs and benefits of work.

And nested council democracy means proportionate decision-making and a sensible approach to meetings and time in general.

So, assuming that in the coming chapters we can fill out its definition and substantiate our claims for it, balanced job complexes will be a worthy structural choice for production (and also consumption) because it is by its very definition and by the dynamics it imposes fully self-managed, capable of diversity, equitable in job assignments, and compatible with material equity and solidarity, assuming, that is, that we can also build those features into allocation.

Balanced job complexes are, moreover, a classless choice—with no systematic difference in power and reward and therefore no class differences among actors in workplaces—and is therefore a good choice for our new economic vision, again, supposing we can make it work in its own right, and along with viable, compatible allocation institutions.

ALLOCATION

First we ought to consider markets, for now without too much detail. What do we mean by markets?

- That all goods, including labor, are bought and sold for prices set competitively.

- That each actor tries to maximize his or her own gain and that no actor can advance without it being at the competitive expense of some other actor.

- That decisions are all made in light of immediate effects on personal well-being for consumers and institutional profit for producers—since to do otherwise is to suffer unnecessarily as a consumer or risk being competed right out of business as a producer.

- That since workplace decisions are purely technical, seeking only to maximize revenues minus costs without taking account of the social needs of workers or of the community or even of consumers, they are best left to administrators. (In other words, even if workers have power, they will cede it to a class of coordinators, as in Yugoslavia, via what we have called formal but unimplemented workers control, rather than preside over decisions to oppress themselves. Workers won't want to or have the freedom from impacts to decide how to restrict their own options, to push themselves beyond what is comfortable, to reduce their own incomes, to reduce product quality against the interests of consumers, to ignore pollution affects on the community, etc., all to lower costs and raise revenues, but will instead hire managers to make these alienated decisions for them.)

Moreover, we know both by our ability to analyze their intrinsic dynamics and by looking at history, that as a result of the operations of markets, a market economy inevitably has:

- Commodity fetishism—wherein decisions account for prices of things but take little account of social relations between people.

- Antagonistic roles—wherein I get ahead at your loss and solidarity is destroyed.

- Anti-social bias—wherein goods are inevitably mispriced such that those which benefit groups are under valued and thereby under produced, while those that help individuals but at a cost to non-buyers are over valued and thereby over produced, all leading to an anti-social pattern of production and investment and an ensuing personality development that is individualist in the narrowest sense.

- Workplace hierarchy—wherein a coordinator class or perhaps a coordinator class and a capitalist class dominate workers.

- Ecological decay—wherein resources are undervalued, pollution and other environmental degradation is minimized, long term effects are left out of decisions, and of course independent ecological criteria can never be taken into account unless they are consistent with simple profit-maximization.

Though there are other problems as well, on any of these grounds, which sound abstract when presented so succinctly but yield the kind of depravity we see throughout our society—poverty, profit-seeking, homelessness, greed, anti-social individuality, unemployment, a few percent of all people owning grossly disproportionate wealth, ecological disasters, and which obviously conflict with all four of our guiding evaluative criteria. Therefore, we can reject markets as an allocation system for our visionary economy.

And now we have some questions to consider based on the discussion to this point:

- Explain structurally how markets impact on people's personalities and preferences?

- Do markets deliver what we want, or do we want what markets deliver, and what difference does it make?

Next, we need to consider central planning. Well, right off we know that:

- Central planning is a system whereby planners (coordinators) in some sort of central planning board determine prices and amounts to be produced in accord with a socially decided set of criteria, or, more often, their own whim and interests.

- Under central planning, in order that the workplaces can be dealt with by the planners and to have someone accountable in each, the planners extend themselves out into the workplaces as a layer of managers, engineers, and so on—the rest of the coordinator class.

And we also know that as a result of the operations of central planning, a centrally planned economy inevitably has:

- Authoritarianism—wherein down go orders, up comes clarification of potentials, down go new orders, and up comes obedience.

- Alienation—wherein, as with markets, there is no way for anyone to account for anyone else's social circumstances because only prices are available for judgment.

- Not self-management in proportion to effect—since even if the planners used a vote to set the criteria by which they plan, at best that's one person, one vote which is a far cry from my having more say in what effects me more and less in what effects you more.

• Investment to enhance coordinator power and wealth—
with an emphasis on centralism, large-scale, and high
tech—regardless of effects on others and on the ecology.

Again it sounds pretty abstract, but in practice it is the disastrous dynamics we saw in the Soviet and other Eastern Bloc economies. So, I think we can reject central planning too.

What about complete decentralization and no allocation among separate locales? How do we evaluate it? Each region is separate and self-sufficient. Economic relations are reduced to community barter, with no significant allocation system to speak of. How does it measure up by our preferred values?

What's left is participatory planning. We are of course going to spend considerable time conceptualizing this last allocation option in the chapters to come, but, for the sake of completeness, and with comparable brevity, we know that it embodies:

• A network of nested councils for consumption and production units, industries, neighborhoods, regions, and so on.

• Facilitation boards to assist in data handling.

• Qualitative information and prices that reveal the true social costs and benefits of alternative choices.

• Remuneration according to effort which, along with balanced job complexes insures comparable consumption bundles and material conditions.

• A generalized and ultimate interest in the total social product and improved average work conditions, even beyond one's local circumstances.

• And an iterated planning procedure in which units communicate their desires back and forth for a number of rounds of revision arriving at an agreed social plan.

In participatory planning workers and consumers express their desires, efficiently modify them in light of ever fuller information concerning their implications for others, and finally, democratically settle on an equitable plan.

Social interaction permits all actors to evaluate the full social burdens and benefits of their own and other people's proposals. Consumption and work equilibrate as consumers discover whose requests require more than average social sacrifice, and workers discover who is proposing to shoulder less than average social burdens. Each participant influences decisions in proportion as he or she is affected by them.

Allocation involves a new social, iterative procedure that differs fundamentally from central planning and markets. Each council assesses past experience and an accumulated record of prior planning to estimate the kinds of efforts others would have to expend to provide a proposed list of inputs, and the uses to which others could put a proposed list of outputs, and then makes its own initial proposal. After seeing all initial proposals, each council gets new information about the effects for others of different options. New estimates of the social values of goods in turn facilitate revising requests until a workable plan is achieved.

In a nutshell, the procedure moves us from an incompatible set of optimal desires to a mutually compatible group of economic choices in two ways:

1. Pressure is brought to bear on consumers requesting more than others and on producers proposing to work less than others to make their proposals more equitable.

2. Revisions of the valuations of goods induce actors to shift away from using scarce resources and goods burdensome to produce and toward using more plentiful resources and goods less burdensome to produce.

Both kinds of focusing move us from incompatible to compatible proposals. The first kind promotes equitable outcomes and the second promotes social efficiency.

Some final questions arise:

• If the above is an account of participatory planning, what might be our evaluation of it by our criteria—or what questions about it do we need to answer to evaluate it?

• How do we evaluate capitalism as we know it in developed economies?

• What about social democracy (and what is it, compared to the Canadian or U.S. economies)?

• What about a market, state ownership, formal workplace democracy system (sometimes, wrongly, called market socialism, more aptly called market coordinatorism, I think). Or a centrally planned, state ownership, hierarchical workplace, Soviet-style economy (or what I call centrally planned coordinatorism)? Or a Green decentralized economy?

• And why might we have hope for something better than the above options?

ANSWERS TO QUESTIONS

"The legitimate purpose of abstraction in social science is never to get away from the real world but rather to isolate certain aspects of the real world for intensive investigation. When, therefore, we say that we are operating at a high level or abstraction, we mean that we are dealing with a relatively small number of aspects of reality; we emphatically do not mean that those aspects with which we are dealing are not capable of historical investigation and factual illustration."

—Paul Sweezy

• Beyond some vague notion of equity what should be the actual criteria of remuneration and disposition of economic responsibilities?

This was a thought question, the answer to which doesn't arise in the book until later. Possibilities would be that we should remunerate for property held, productive output, the value of one's contribution, prior education, skills, effort, sacrifice, or need. Choosing among these depends in part on one's aims, of course, but also on a clear understanding of the implications of each for the values we hold dear. You might want to think about this, preparatory to future discussions.

• We have deduced the possibility of 3x3x4 = 36 different conceivable economic systems including unique combinations of the components. How come we are able to boil this down to only four broad economic types?

Because most of the combinations are not viable.

The idea is simple enough. If we are putting together a stereo system from components, each has to have requirements and implications compatible with the context established by other components. We can't have speakers that require a whole lot of power, and an amp that gives off very little power, for example.

It is similar in an economy. For example, you cannot have markets or central planning and non-hierarchical work places because these allocation systems impose hierarchy on workplaces and don't operate properly in its absence. This is most of the answer, the rest is that I cheated. That is, I left out some conceivable options. For example, private ownership plus central planning by the state (generally called a fascist economy) was left out.

• Who advocates these different models, and why?

Beyond academics playing games, people advocate visions because they want the outcomes those visions promise to deliver. Those who think they will wind up owning the means of production will most aggressively advocate capitalism. They will also try to convince others of its value (by hook or crook).

Those who think they will wind up coordinators will most aggressively advocate coordinator economic systems (usually called, misleadingly, to entice other supporters, "market socialism" or "centrally planned socialism").

Politically identified élites (fascists and Stalinists) will prefer variants on capitalism or coordinatorism in which a one party state runs the show by monopolizing planning posts in the government.

Ultimately, I would argue, working people will most aggressively advocate participatory economics, it being a system that elevates them to optimal status as the only economic actors and thus the dominant ones, as well.

This is all, of course, a bit oversimplified as one may be ignorant of an option or prefer the least evil, having ruled out the best option as impossible—the excuse given by many who profess left values but advocate market coordinatorism despite its many failings.

• What are the class relations of each of the four models and how do they arise from the basic institutions employed?

The ownership relations and hierarchical production relations of capitalism generate a three tiered class structure of capitalists (owning the means of production), coordinators (monopolizing knowledge and skills and job slots prerequisite to control over not only their own economic circumstances, but those of others lacking these claims), and workers (who simply sell their ability to do work for a wage and follow out orders given by others, carving out the best existence possible by organizing to increase their bargaining power).

With the private ownership of capital eliminated in the post capitalist societies that I call coordinatorist, the remaining allocation and production relations demarcate two classes, coordinators and workers, and elevate the former to dominance over the latter.

In participatory economics, or "parecon" for short, there is no class distinction generated by ownership, production, or allocation relations (not consumption either), and, on the contrary, these aspects of economic life all generate classless dynamics.

- Explain structurally how markets impact on people's personalities and preferences?

This is a big and a bit unfair question.

Briefly, markets compel us to consider our own well-being and ignore (as well as be ignorant of) the well-being of those who produce what we consume or consume what we produce. We will try to fulfill ourselves in consumption and due to the biased pricing of products under market allocation—those that are private will be under-priced and those that are public will be over-priced—we will, in reaction, bend ourselves to prefer the former.

Instead of markets delivering what people want, therefore, people come to want what markets deliver. Thus our beings follow a trajectory of preference development that arises outside ourselves in the dynamics of markets and profit of the few. We become self-centered and egocentric due to market impositions, rather than markets delivering ever more egocentric and self-centered products because the drive for these is built into our beings.

- Do markets deliver what we want, or do we want what markets deliver, and what difference does it make?

If markets delivered what we want, with no ill effects along the way, they would be a kind of neutral conveyor belt of economic life, letting us manifest our preferences freely. Our beings and preferences would be determinant.

In the second possibility, regardless of who we are and what we might want in the most free conditions, markets would contour us in predictable ways. In other words markets will cause us to evolve preferences for what markets are biased to deliver to us. These results are aggravated when markets are combined with private ownership, but exist even when property is socialized, but markets are retained.

To understand this dynamic, think in terms of someone being deposited in prison and developing (sensibly) a taste for what the prison commissary has to offer—though, if the same person were outside the prison, he or she would dismiss all the offerings as horrible, not distinguishing among them. The prisoner reconstructs his or her preferences so as to get the best out of what is available. Notice then that what is made available is critical to the prisoner's evolving preferences, as are the prices attached. If some things are under priced and others over priced relative to their true worth, we incline toward developing preferences for the former and away from the latter.

Markets do not just make any old thing available, and only at correct prices. Rather they impose biases into what is provided and at what prices, and we then operate in context of these biases (just as the prisoner operates in context of the limited offerings of the commissary) and the result is that we learn to like what is available, rather than what is available coming into accord with what we freely want. This is the difference between freedom and alienation.

> • What about complete decentralization and no allocation
> among separate regions. How do we evaluate it?

Many people argue for this but to me, to be blunt, it is an idiotic notion. Not that there isn't a kernel of wisdom in it. Yes, face to face relations are sometimes preferable to larger scale arrangements. And if we make these face to face structures democratic and participatory, that's all the better. But "small is good" is not some kind of unbridgeable principle. It will be valid when a smaller approach is the better way to attain aims like justice, equity, solidarity, diversity, ecological balance, efficient use of productive assets, and so on. But when a smaller approach doesn't better propel these ends, then small is a bad choice. Elaborated into an entire economic vision—little self-sufficient communities acting in isolation from one another—"small is beautiful" means either gargantuan redundancy of effort and huge inefficiencies, waste, and ecological harm; or extreme deprivation. It also means, inevitably, gross inequality between regions that have different local assets (and to redress this by allocation is to argue for a different model).

Opting a priori for small seems also to curtail diversity and variety, and to even be inconsistent with the idea of universal interdependence of all living actors and their environments that is generally typical of ecological thought.

What is sought in this vision—ecological balance, participation, no alienation, etc.—is not, in fact, attained. So why people advocate the view is a bit of a mystery to me. It seems almost like an intellectual fetish, incompletely thought out.

- If the above (in the chapter) is an account of participatory planning, what might be our evaluation of it by our criteria—what questions about it do we need to design to evaluate it?

It seems to me that if the brief description I offered in our multi-economy discussion was valid, then we would know that parecon fulfilled the values we set out for a visionary economy. The questions, of course, are can it actually work? What are the details? Why won't it just collapse in chaos or stasis?

- How do we evaluate capitalism as we know it in our own experiences?

It is, by our criteria of judgment, a dung heap. It destroys solidarity, creates inequity unparalleled in history, gives some people almost unlimited power over outcomes while denying most people even marginal say over their own economic circumstances, and it even distorts personalities and preferences in such ways as to homogenize outcomes and reduce diversity. The fact that most academics would be horrified by my terminology—"it is a dung heap"—is no testament to their civility or integrity.

- What about social democracy (and what is it, compared to the Canadian and U.S. economies, for example)?

Social Democracy is capitalism with a more powerful working class (and coordinator class) and a weaker capitalist class. It is, as a result, better, with a variety of reform structures incorporated to ameliorate and even, in some instances, redress problems arising from the underlying capitalist structure. It is a quite unstable economic structure, however, as a shift in balance of economic power can quickly cause revision to more aggressive capitalist dynamics (as in Sweden and Scandinavia more generally, in the 1990s). The structure is capitalism, but the balance of power between classes is less favorable to those at the top.

- What about a market, state ownership, formal workplace democracy system (sometime, wrongly, called market socialism, more aptly called market coordinatorism, I think). Or a centrally planned, state ownership, hierarchical workplace, Soviet-style economy (or what I call centrally planned coordinatorism)? Or a Green decentralized economy?

The answers follow from our evaluations of the components of each model. Having rejected markets and central planning and complete decentralism, etc., we reject these systems as being flawed by inclusion of these components.

- And why might we have hope for something better than the above options?

Either because we have thought long and hard on the issues and decided that some alternative arrangement has much better qualities and is possible, or because we have no compelling answers of that type but we realize that without hope for something better, we will only get worse. This latter, I suppose, is a kind of religious belief and historically it is not so easy to say which type of hope serves a progressive movement better. I myself think having both types at once is a nice combination.

3. Production Values

What are our guiding aims for how we organize work?

"As it happens, there are no columns in standard double-entry book-keeping to keep track of satisfaction and demoralization. There is no credit entry for feelings of self-worth and confidence, no debit column for feelings of uselessness and worthlessness. There are no monthly, quarterly, or even annual statements of pride and no closing statement of bankruptcy when the worker finally comes to feel that after all he couldn't do anything else, and doesn't deserve anything better."

—Barbara Garson

In this chapter we are going to try to refine our general values into a set of more precise requirements for production relations and workplaces generally.

Production Values

So, what norms do we want to have guide our design of workplace relationships? Well, we know from the prior discussions we have had that my answer is equity (of material and circumstances), solidarity, diversity, and participatory self-management, plus efficiency (in the sense of attaining desired outcomes with as little waste as possible). But what does this set of aims translate into in a workplace environment? What, more specifically and precisely, are our goals for workplace life?

I want to point out, as a kind of sidebar, that you should see the methodology at work here. It's obvious and easy, once one gets into it. If you want to follow along using other values that you prefer to those I am using in the following chapters, by all means do so. First, establish general values. Apply them in specific contexts to get more refined and specific goals. Then move on (as we'll do in later chapters) to actually designing systems to attain the goals. Be sure your choices are compatible, from one domain to another.

A workplace involves tasks that need to be done and decisions that need to be made. There will be a host of roles people fill which is what makes it an institution, in my view. And so the question becomes, what goals do we have for those roles (in light of the need to get work done and decisions made) to meet our overarching aims of equity, solidarity, diversity, and self-management, plus minimizing waste (of things we care about)?

So let's take each value in turn, and assess its broad implications for production relations.

Equity

Equity, remember, doesn't mean a fair race. Instead it refers to fair outcomes. So what does it say to us about workplace role structures, for example?

Somehow, it must be that in each workplace what people do is fairly apportioned. What you do, and what I do has to be seen as fair, by our standards, in every workers' eyes. More, this is true if we are in the same work team in a workplace, if we are in the same workplace but don't have the same responsibilities, and even if we are in different workplaces, across town from one another, or in San Francisco, on the one hand, and Toronto, on the other.

Well, the possibilities for role defining would seem to be:

1. Apportion responsibilities so we all do exactly the same exact things as one another at work under the same exact conditions.

2. Apportion responsibilities so we all work the same length of time, but we do whatever we are best at.

3. Let everyone do whatever they want, for however long they want to do it.

4. Let everyone judge the available options and negotiate with one another for who does what, and then work the same amount of time as one another.

5. Divide up stuff into jobs all of whose responsibilities require some fixed level of background or skill and maximally utilize it, and then have people compete for who gets what jobs, but have all work the same length day.

6. Do either of the prior three options, but juggle the time required at work to offset any differences in job quality by requiring extra or less time on the job depending as one's work situation is better or worse.

7. Apportion tasks into jobs that are comparable in their quality of life impact, and let everyone then negotiate for who gets to have which jobs, all worked the same length of time per day.

And, perhaps, you can think of some other options as well.

The questions that arise are:

- How do we rate these options (and any others you wish to add) if we are taking into account only equity? Which options are equitable, and which aren't? Why? Remember, we are only talking about equity, at this point.

- How might we refine our equity aim regarding workplaces and production?

SOLIDARITY

A condition of solidarity—as we will define it—is that people care about each other's well-being and assess their own actions in part in light of the effects on others. Optimally, it includes a high degree of empathy.

So, again, we have the problem of figuring out what kind of relations among actors, what kind of apportionment of tasks among them, and what kind of distribution of decision making power are consistent with promoting solidarity, and what kinds are contrary to promoting solidarity?

Before you get irritated about my approach to piling on these questions, please remember this is a book about conceptualizing new economic models, not about learning a particular one or merely hearing an argument in favor of this or that perspective. If you don't try to do some conceptualizing, well, you aren't going to get as much out of this book. And, anyhow, I will also provide answers, all in good time. So:

- Think in terms of roles, as in the above list under the equity issue, but also think in terms of distribution of decision making power and actual interactions among actors, and try to enunciate a variety of options, and their merits and debits vis-à-vis solidarity, and, for the purposes of this question, only solidarity.
- Refine our aim for solidarity into workplace aims.

DIVERSITY

Diversity is simply a condition of many outcomes, many approaches to accomplishing ends, many variants and circumstances which one can either choose among, at different times, or benefit vicariously from, via the different effects on others, or seeing others in different forms of action.

- With the seven forms of workplace organization listed earlier, and any others you might care to evaluate, consider the implications for diversity of outcomes.

PARTICIPATORY SELF-MANAGEMENT

We have already refined this into a notion that immediately translates to production and the workplace. We want each actor to have a say in outcomes proportionate to the effects the outcomes have on that actor. Can we translate this more, in light of the details of the workplace context?

- What does our self-management aim tell us about one person, one vote in the work place? Think about some decisions and whether it makes sense that everyone have equal say and everyone vote.

- What does it tell us about power being vested in the hands of only a subset of the employees?

- What does it tell us about limits on the worker's impact on decisions—vis-à-vis community residents and consumers?

- Finally, if you can rule out some options for workplace organization in light of our self-management aim, can you also say anything positive or prescriptive about what we might incorporate into workplace decision making to meet this aim? Either institutions or methods?

EFFICIENCY

Remember, the idea of efficiency is that we don't want to set a goal for the actions of a workplace and then meet that goal, but in a way that wastes things we care about in the process (time, materials of value, energy, whatever).

On the other hand, efficiency does not mean that the only thing that matters is quantities we can enumerate on some scale of measurement.

- So what does the efficiency aim tell us about meeting all the other aims that we also have? Do any of your ideas about the implications of the other values for workplace organization and institutions and decision making come into conflict with the desire to avoid needless waste? Do they facilitate efficiency in the best sense of the term?

ANSWERS TO QUESTIONS

"How many care to seek only for precedents? How many fiery innovators are mere copycats of bygone revolutionaries?"

—Peter Kropotkin

The topic of this chapter is production values and we began by discussing the norms we want for our design of workplace relationships. We started with equity (of material and circumstances), solidarity, diversity, and participatory self-management, plus efficiency (in the sense of attaining desired outcomes with as little waste as possible) and we tried to move from these broad aims to more specific aims for workplaces.

To do this we listed seven ways of dividing up tasks in the workplace. And over the course of the chapter I requested that you evaluate these from the perspective of our values. Here are my brief responses, then:

- Apportion responsibilities so we all do the same exact things as one another at work under the same exact conditions.

In the abstract, I guess I would say this is pretty equitable. Everyone gets the same circumstances. Likewise there is no hierarchy, though I am not sure how decisions would be made. I don't know whether there is a solidarity of misery or not. There is no diversity.

In practice, it is of course absurd. First, there is no such thing as allotting work so that each thing to be done is divided into identical tasks for all people in the workplace. But even ignoring problems like that, the other difficulty is that while abstractly equitable, the option pays no attention to the unique interests, desires, and potentials of the actors. I guess someone might like the peculiar combination of things they would have to do, but most people wouldn't, to differing degrees. Anyhow, this is really pretty stupid. It is equitable, in a sense, but horribly inefficient due to misusing everyone's unique capacities.

- Apportion responsibilities so we all work the same length of time, but do whatever we are best at.

The idea here is supposed to be that the only things that matter are (a) how long we work, and (b) how much we produce.

How long matters, in this view, because we all so uniformly and completely dislike work that doing one thing or another makes little difference. The only thing that matters to us is when we get off. How much we produce matters, however, because our boss wants profits, or society wants more output.

As to being equitable, assuming that with this option we actually wind up doing only what we are best at, unless the claim about everyone hating all work equally is correct, equity disappears. One person is best at something pleasant, another person happens to excel at something quite onerous. Likewise for some winding up with more power, and some with less due to what they are best at, precluding self-management and solidarity. There could be variety, however.

- Let everyone do whatever they want, for however long they want to do it.

This option is strange to evaluate on equity grounds. If we are all doing precisely what we want, to the degree we want, it is hard to see how we could call it inequitable. After all, you couldn't change its equity characteristics, or any other characteristics, without forcing someone to make a choice other than what they already preferred.

It seems obvious, doesn't it?

However, a problem arises. What jobs do people choose from? I have fudged the issue by not commenting on this in the definition. We can't each do whatever we want, or there will be no output because what you want, what I want, and what she and he want may not match up together. If I want to go left on the assembly line and you want to go right, or I want to do one sequence for some function, and you want a different sequence, we get a mess. So presumably this option comes down to meaning that from among the available job options, we each do what we want. Well that sounds nice, but what if we all want one option, and not any other? So it might mean from among all the options, subject to the constraint that things get done, we each pick what we want. Well, that sounds fine, but when our choices won't get stuff done, who changes? And, most important and least often addressed, who (or what) sets up the options to choose from in the first place?

Without more detail this seemingly ideal option may not be equitable, certainly says nothing about self-management (even though it seems to emphasize that), will be diverse, however, and if it fails on any other counts, won't be solidaritous.

- Let everyone judge the available options and negotiate with one another for who does what, and then work the same amount of time as one another.

This seems pretty good, at first glance. But again, we have this problem of where the options that we negotiate among came from. If they are very unequal, then however we decide to divide them up, someone gets a raw deal and equity is gone. More, if we didn't set them, then we aren't self managing. If they aren't unequal, however, and we did decide the options, well, then we may be unto something.

- Divide up stuff into jobs all of whose responsibilities require some fixed level of background or skill and maximally utilize it, and then have people compete for who gets what jobs, while all work the same length day.

This is what advocates of market post capitalist economies advocate, I believe. The market induces this type of job structure, and this type of competition. The outcome is inequitable by virtue of different people enjoying or suffering differential quality of life at work, and is obviously also anti-solidaritous as people compete for better circumstances, and it fails to have self-management as well, as some jobs will have power over others.

- Do either of the prior three options, but juggle the time required at work to offset any differences in job quality by requiring extra or less time on the job depending as one's work situation is better or worse.

If we are talking simply equity, I think this is hard to criticize. Thus, I say I will do the harder, more onerous job, but I want more pay for it or to work less hours for the same income. The idea is that we balance not just quality of life at work, but the sum of quality of life at work and quality of life in consumption. If the former is lower, we reward more income so the latter can make up for it. This option is not to be sneered at, I think, so long as we are only talking equity. Notice, it means the person in the pleasant or uplifting job gets less pay than the person in the dangerous or boring one.

And this option certainly allows diversity and doesn't have to preclude solidarity either, it would seem. But on self-management grounds it likely fails. For if people are choosing among options that have widely differing empowerment effects, then even if we balance for quality of life by rewarding those who take the less fulfilling or more onerous jobs with more income, the differential impact on people's abilities to participate in decisions, on their knowledge and skills, and so on, will mean a divergence from self-management. A group will rise to positions of dominance in decision making, and then, in time, will decide to redesign the remuneration scheme in its own interest.

- Apportion tasks into jobs that are comparable in their quality of life impact, and let everyone then negotiate for who gets to have which jobs, while everyone works the same length of time per day.

This seems rather equitable. By the way we define the jobs, the outcomes are equitable. By the way we choose jobs, we preserve diversity and allow for the possibility of self-management. Absent inequality and competition, solidarity is also possible.

We can also be flexible on the hours, rewarding more or less income as one chooses to work more or less hours.

- Refine our aim for solidarity into workplace aims.

What does this mean?

Well, we say we want the economy to promote solidarity. So, what does that mean in a workplace? What conditions promote solidarity? It seems to me that the answer to this is that we need a workplace organization and process which gives each worker empathy for the situation of others, gives each an interest in all others having as good a situation as oneself, and gives all the workers an interest in innovation that doesn't pit different groups against one another.

This idea is simple enough, once enunciated. An economic institution promotes solidarity to the extent that it gives people interests that are compatible, or mutually supportive, or even identical. You get ahead, I get ahead, and vice versa. Also, to the extent the structures give each worker a sense of what others do, and a respect for their contribution, this too will augment solidarity.

Suppose in my workplace we are deciding between two possible innovations—one affects the quality of life in the foundry, the other affects it in the promotion department. What is the solidaritous dynamic, and the anti-solidaritous dynamic for resolving this choice?

We said in chapter 3, also, that we want each actor to have a say in outcomes proportionate to the effects the outcomes have on that actor.

- What does our self-management aim tell us about one person, one vote in the work place?

It tells us it is nonsense. We don't have each person vote equally on when I will go to the bathroom, or whether you will put your phone on the right hand or the left hand side of your desk. Why? Because these decisions don't impact everyone to the same extent, nor do all but a very few decisions, in fact, which is what one person, one vote does. Assessing this is as easy as pie. We easily eliminate this option for decision making, taken as a general rule, as incompatible with our goal. The hard part is to register this, and to then abide it, not continually glancing back and saying, OK, let's decide by one person, one vote.

- What does it tell us about power being vested in the hands of only a subset of the employees?

This is obviously ruled out as well. If a subset of workers have power, then unless one believes decisions impact only on them, one has abrogated the goal of each actor having a say in decisions proportionate to the effect of the decisions on them. Obviously it isn't only a few people in the workplace who are affected by decisions about how everyone works, with what tools, at what pace, making what products, and so on. So, another option is eliminated.

- What does it tell us about limits on the worker's impact on decisions vis-à-vis community residents and consumers?

Well, if people in neighborhoods or consumers wherever they may be are also to have proportionate say in decisions depending on the extent they are affected by them, clearly they will have to have input, by one means or another, in many decisions about the workplace. To rule them out is itself ruled out by our goal.

- Finally, I asked if you can rule out some options for workplace organization in light of our self-management aim, can you also say anything positive or prescriptive about what we might incorporate into workplace decision making to meet this aim? Either institutions or methods?

I will answer this from my perspective later.

- I also asked, however, what does the efficiency aim tell us about meeting all the other aims that we also have? Do any of your ideas about the implications of the other values for workplace organization and institutions and decision making come into conflict with the desire to avoid needless waste? Do they facilitate efficiency in the best sense of the term?

The answer here is also simple. It depends on what we mean by efficiency. If we mean maximizing output while minimizing (monetary) cost, that is one thing, and it will conflict with many of our other aims.

But if we mean attaining the aims we seek with minimum waste of anything we care about—which is what we ought to mean—then it is merely a shorthand way of evaluating our attainment of all our other values.

One of the major achievements of bourgeois propaganda has been to establish the idea that economics is about quantities and particularly profits—thus the strange and horrible meaning given to the term efficiency. If, instead, we say economics is about meeting people's needs and developing their potentials, then, of course, we get a very different definition of efficiency. Efficient for one goal, an economy will be inefficient for many others.

There is another way to understand this strangeness about the economics profession. Imagine, for a moment, that we create a scholastic department in universities throughout the country whose purpose is to comprehend and teach about human procreation. Now imagine that these departments developed an extensive toolbox of concepts and analyses for the purpose, and that these made no reference to the human well-being and development of mothers or children. Instead, they focus only on, say, the amount of oxygen or other nutrients used during the birthing process and other chemical phenomena. This would surely be strange. Or imagine a scholastic study of medicine which paid lots of attention to the techniques, the biological theories, the buildings and tools, but said almost nothing about the effect of medicine on sick people. While not exactly analogous to the economics profession, these failings are similar to studying economics without concepts that focus on the affects of economic structures and choices on economic actors, particularly workers. And so it is that the word efficiency comes to have no connection whatever to the human implications of economic activity—save in the sense that maximizing profits itself has, of course, many human implications.

4. Consumption Values

What are our broad aims for consumption?

"All who are not lunatics are agreed about certain things. That it is better to be alive than dead, better to be adequately fed than starved, better to be free than a slave. Many people desire those things only for themselves and their friends; they are quite content that their enemies should suffer. These people can be refuted by science: Humankind has become so much one family that we cannot insure our own prosperity except by insuring that of everyone else. If you wish to be happy yourself, you must resign yourself to seeing others also happy."

—Bertrand Russell

In this chapter we do for consumption what we did for production last chapter: move from our general encompassing values to more precise evaluative norms and aims for consumption per se.

Consumption Values

Consumption is not something I think it makes sense to beat to death. We each consume for our own reasons. To enjoy, learn, whatever. And the economist isn't supposed to try to second guess our reasons. But an economist should note that we need to remove biases built into the economic structures that distort or otherwise constrain our preferences, and we need to be sure that the value of what each person is free to consume is such that the overall impact is to promote our favored values. In this chapter we seek to refine our goals, this time for consumption, beyond the very general aims of equity, self-management, solidarity, diversity, and efficiency.

So the real focus for this discussion needs to be income, or how much we deserve to consume; what we as consumers need to have in order to be able to do our consuming—however much it is—responsibly; and how much control we should have over what we get.

How much does each person get to have out of the total that is produced by all people's work? What information does each person need, to make sensible consumption choices? What determines what is available and therefore how much say do we each have over what we get, including over what is available?

Think of income as a claim on social product. Whatever income you get, or I get, or anyone gets, indicates what proportion of the product you, I, or anyone is entitled to have. The idea is we can each have a bundle of stuff whose value has to equal the amount our income says we are entitled to. As to how this allocation occurs and how we can measure this value, that comes later. For now the question is, instead, what share in the whole should we each have?

Historically there are not too many answers offered for this question.

1. One possibility is that we are entitled to a share based on how much everything that we own produces—including not only our own labor, but our land, our machines, and so on. What our property produces determine what share of the social product we deserve to consume.

2. Second, we might receive a share based on what each individual actually contributes to the social product. If I produce more, I get back more. If I produce less, I get back less.

3. Next, perhaps we each just get whatever we can manage to grab. What we get, we get, by hook or crook, however much we or our property might produce—perhaps with a few laws limiting our methods.

4. Another possibility is that we receive according to our needs. Who needs more, gets more. Who needs less, gets less.

5. Finally, another possibility is that we receive in proportion to the effort and sacrifice we offer up in our work. Not the amount we produce, but the amount we labor.

So, we all now know the evaluative drill.

• How do we feel about these options? These are the ones economists discuss. We have some overarching values. So which of these do we like, and why? And which do we reject, and why?

Before we figure out actual institutional structures for a good economy, we have to know, in some more detail than just broad sweeping goals, what we want them to accomplish. And that is what we were up to last chapter, and now this chapter too.

But what about the second issue raised above. What information do you need as a consumer to be able to do your consuming effectively and responsibly?

Again, we can think of some possibilities:

1. We arguably need to know our own preferences. What do we want? This is probably not controversial, but we might wonder whether it is always possible, in all economies. That is, what has to be true of the economy for us to be able to know this with some confidence?

2. We also need to know what is available and what its value is so we can make our choices in a way that adds up to at most the total value of product we are entitled to. Sure, but what does it mean to say we need to know the value of each item?

And:

• Is this enough? Would it be sufficient to know our own needs and desires, honestly and fully, and to know what things cost (accurately, unlike in our current system)? Or is there other knowledge we should have if we are to make responsible and sensible decisions about consumption, in a way promoting the values we want our economy to attain?

• What about qualitative knowledge of material inputs and outputs, or qualitative knowledge of human effects, or of byproducts and their effects? Is this all just redundant, once we have good prices? Or do we need this level of knowledge as well as prices?

• Finally, how much say should each person have over what they consume?

• Do we just get what we say we want, with the sole constraint being that it is consistent with our income?

• Or should the make up of our returns be influenced by people who are affected by how we live our lives, in turn affected by what we consume? And if so, what does this translate to as a guideline? Think about alcohol.

• And what should be the relation between group needs and individual needs in the process of arriving at outcomes?

• Now, finally, in light of all your answers, can you describe the income norms, information norms, and power norms of consumption as we know it in our society, and as you would like it, in brief summary, noting the difference.

Please notice, this whole discussion should not occur at the level of we are too consumerist, or we eat too much, or such like. The volume of our consumption is not really the point here, or how much we do of it. You might want to indicate why that is.

Well, there are quite a few questions here. But, if you have the time for it, please try to answer for yourself before reading on. Try also to use only what we have already covered in answering the questions. And don't despair. Soon we will come to institutions.

ANSWERS TO QUESTIONS

"Concepts which have proved useful for ordering things easily assume so great an authority over us, that we forget their terrestrial origin and accept them as unalterable facts. They then become labeled as ' conceptual necessities,' etc. The road of scientific progress is frequently blocked for long periods by such errors. It is therefore not just an idle game to exercise our ability to analyze familiar concepts, and to demonstrate the conditions on which this justification of their usefulness depends."

—Albert Einstein

For chapter 4, the focus has been on consumption values. How do we translate our overarching norms—equity, solidarity, self-management, diversity, and efficiency—into a set of more explicit aims regarding consumption? And what do we get when we do this? So here are my answers to the questions I raised.

OPTIONS FOR INCOME EVALUATED

How do we feel about the options that have historically been offered?

- It could be that we each have claims on output in proportion to how much of the means of production we own, or how productive the means of production we own are.

This option yields differential income with no basis in anything that the individuals involved have actually done or committed of themselves. It is inequitable in the same way that it is inequitable if you give one child a very narrow straw, and another a wide straw, and set them both to the task of drinking out of a single milk glass, day in and day out for breakfast.

As with the children, division according to capital ownership is not conducive to solidarity since jealousy and attempts to grab the bigger straw get in the way.

More, basing income on property owned ensures that those with high income will use it to enhance their abilities to control other choices—who gets which toys, and, even more important, who gets the next technical innovation, especially the next bit of additional productive property, thus also violating self-management in a progressive spiral of divergence from proportionate say for all actors over the decisions affecting their lives.

Regarding diversity, the option has relatively minor implications, beyond narrowing options for some.

As to efficiency, the option does foster the most profitable use of capital goods for the owner. But it doesn't lead to the widest possible development and utilization of people's talents and abilities.

- Or it could be that we each have claims on output in proportion to how much of it we are ourselves responsible for producing.

This is a very popular conception, including among people who call themselves socialists. If you produce more of the overall output of society than I do, you should have just that much more claim on the social product. Or so goes the argument.

But what determines the gap between what you produce and what I produce? It could be ownership of better tools, unless we have already ruled that out, as above. But it could also be that you work harder. Or that you have better training. Or that you are just plain more productive, intrinsically, because independent of how hard we work or how much training we have, you are quicker, stronger, calculate faster, have a better eye for design, or whatever.

Should such differences be rewarded? Let's leave out of consideration the work harder component of the difference in output for now, dealing with it below, to consider first genetic endowment.

Let's say we are picking oranges. If you are physically bigger and stronger, and we work equally hard and for an equal period of time, should you get more reward because your pile of oranges is bigger than mine? Well, to reward this is to say that hey, since you were already lucky in the genetic lottery, now we will bestow on you some more advantage to go with what that luck already gave you. What justice is there in this? And it can't be a matter of incentives, as opposed to justice, for surely no matter how much or in what manner we set up our payment schemes, no one is going to be able to respond by improving their genetic endowment. There is no incentive effect on attributes that are beyond our control. And there is no moral reason to reward what we have nothing to do with determining either. So the option is inequitable and without redeeming worth.

But what about differences in skill and knowledge that are learned rather than inherited. Suppose I go to school for four years while you sweat in a mine. Then we both work someplace where my school training makes me more productive. Do I deserve to be paid more? First, I enjoyed my school days while you enhanced your probability of dying of black lung. Then I benefit again on top of that when I work at the same effort level as you, because my learned skills increase my output.

What's the logic? It can't be moral. It can't be that I deserve more for my pleasurable time in school. Incentives you might say. We need to pay for the schooling or else people wouldn't do it. Well, yes, if the schooling is onerous and involves sacrifice and hard work, we ought to pay for that, like we pay for it in any productive contribution because it is deserving and because the incentive effect is needed. But if a task we undertake is pleasant and fulfilling, why do we have to pay a whole bunch extra to get people to do it?

The answer, of course, is that we do not. This is just one more of the almost endless array of idiotic lies hoisted by economists upon the public. Ask yourself, given the choice, would you opt for grad school or a job, say, in a coal mine, for the next 6 years? Suppose the coal miner's pay is $30,000 a year. The incentives argument is that we need to pay you more, over a lifetime, in returns on the schooling, to get you to do it. Well, is this true? Would you do the schooling or the coal mining at $30,000 each? Now, how high do we have to raise the coal mining salary to get you to do it instead of the grad schooling at $30,000?

The deduction is simple. There are elements of schooling and learning skills that should be remunerated, as work, in the same way as more typical work is. But the accumulated skill, talents, and knowledge, which then contributes to output, should not be remunerated per se.

So what are the impacts on solidarity, self-management, diversity, and efficiency? Well, what we are really talking about here, I believe, is a clear class division. A gap created between conceptual and order-giving economic actors and instrumental order-taking actors based on the qualitative effects of their activity, and on the remuneration for it as well. However this gap initially opens up (genetic endowment, training, luck, brute force) once it exists those with power and extra income will use it to further enhance the conditions of their dominance (by setting up associations to keep people out of their profession, establishing school tracking, etc.) thus gaining a disproportionate control over economic outcomes. A class rule is fostered: coordinator class dominance over working class dominated. Solidarity is gone. Diversity is delimited for those at the bottom—and even for those at the top who must defend their positions.

Why then is this choice popular among many who call themselves socialists? Well, I have to say that I think that the answer is either ignorance or that these individuals are bound by, rather than interested in transcending, their class position. They advocate coordinator class vision and values, however unself-consciously, pure and simple. Often they take their stands with a truly caring heart … but then capitalists sometimes show a little heart too, as long as the basic underlying values that keep them on top are preserved.

- Or it could be that we each have claims on output as large as we are able to bargain for, in a competitive negotiation with others.

This is just war by another name. And it is, in fact, what exists in real market economies. Remuneration is a function of such things as monopoly buying or selling power, control over technologies, barriers to entry, organizational might (in unions or corporations), ability to withhold assets and thereby wreck havoc, and so forth. Power, bargaining power to be exact, is the main determinant of income.

There is no equity in any humane sense. More like the law of a nightmare. Solidarity is gone. Self-management is gone.

- Or it could be that we each have any claims on output that we wish to make—we just get whatever we say we want.

And where does it all come from? This is, indeed, utopian. Meaning it is impossible because of limitations built into the domain we are discussing. It is like asking trees to fly.

- Or it could be we each have claims on output in proportion to our needs, as compared to everyone else.

This option is nice too. Indeed, it is really just the previous option, but with a lid on demand. But what is the lid? Where is it established? Is it our needs and wants? If so, how do we measure these, and why is there in fact a lid on our needs and wants? The only way such a lid can arise is if we put limits on ourselves before the fact of knowing what society can deliver, or if we do it in light of understanding what the economy's situation and potential are. How do we curtail ourselves without knowledge of potentials? Does everyone do it the same? Is it even a good idea? If we are curtailing ourselves in light of potentials, we are operating in terms of a budget, and not the above option. These are things to think about because they actually have implications later. The point is, we don't have to spend much time on this option now because surely expressed needs would greatly exceed available output now, so that this option immediately reverts to the prior "get what you want" option or has to be passed over en route to the next option we will consider.

But what if we had socialist (or parecon) people, who had developed a profound social responsibility as a natural part of their beings (much as people now learn quite early how to grab)? Would we then want an economy in which people essentially limit their requests, but get what they say they want? (The only alternative still in the range of this option would be some objective determination of need from without, which would remove control over our lives from us, and is obviously authoritarian.) Would this in fact be good, as many intuitively think (especially Greens)? (I think the answer is no, this would not be ideal.) Anyhow, in the real world, for now and the indefinite future, getting income according to desires is utopian at least if thought of as operating as the sole criterion for allocation of all goods. (Though, say, for health care it might work fine.)

- Or it could be that we each have claims on output in proportion to the effort we expend and the sacrifices we incur in creating output.

This rewards only what we have control over. So as an incentive and as a fair response to our efforts it makes sense. I don't think it would disrupt solidarity, even if some people work a little harder and earn a little more and other people work a little less hard and earn a little less, supposing each person is free to choose any available option. The income differentials couldn't become very large, certainly not large enough to disrupt self-management. All in all, I don't see any problem other than the following:

- What if I can't work? Or what if I have a disease, or a hurricane hits my neighborhood and so I have way more expenses than others?

The answer is to have distribution according to need for calamities, health matters, and some other related similar facets of consumption. Where do these provisions come from? Everything always comes from the overall social product. So, it must be that in our good economy some part of the total social product is set aside for these purposes. It is a kind of social fund, or insurance fund, if you like.

- Or, it could be some combination of the above.

Which is what I arrived at above.

- I also asked: what kind of information must a person have to make sensible decisions about which items they would like to get from amongst all those produced in society, up to their income level? What do our overarching values tell us ought to be our aims in this regard? And I presented some options and urged that each be evaluated.

At a minimum it would seem that we each must at least have knowledge of our own preferences, and of the actual composition of available items to choose, and of their value (so we can sum up the value of all our choices to the limits of our share of the total available output). So, first, we could have only this knowledge in the form of self awareness, some kind of price structure, and some kind of informational advertising.

This doesn't have any first order implications for equity. Using the "price indicators" we can choose consumption goods totaling to our income level, and if that has been determined equitably, we are fine on this score. But the approach doesn't do anything for solidarity, however, and arguably is even anti-solidaritous. Why? Well suppose you were operating in your family and you never took any account of the actual impact of what you are doing on anyone else. It just wasn't an option. Indeed, you could instead only consider implications for yourself. This would clearly not be solidaritous, even if the other family members were recompensed when your choices affected them adversely.

As to self-management and diversity, I think the effects are modest depending on the accuracy of the pricing structure. If the prices reflect true social costs and benefits, when we use them to make our choices we are at least judging in light of a sensible accounting. If they diverge from true social costs and benefits, however, even our best efforts will nonetheless diverge from our true interests. The informative problem about information in this option, however, is that while there is theoretically enough information in a price that represents true social costs and benefits for people to make good choices, there is no information to facilitate that people actually feel any concern or have any empathy for one another. So regardless of their desires, in the absence of this information people have to act as though others do not even exist.

Of course, if the price doesn't account for the full social costs and benefits—the full effects on people and society—then in addition to the problem of the absence of qualitative information, we will have a price that is misleading and our decisions will be inadequate no matter what our motivations may be.

We could add to the prior list of things we need to know, knowledge of what goes into producing the items that we might choose to consume, material inputs, that is.

In other words, we could add to a price some qualitative information about what the material components are. It is progress of a sort, but not much, at least bearing on the question above. We now know that when we buy a bicycle it uses rubber, and so has implications for rubber workers, but we know nothing about the circumstances of those workers.

- We could add knowledge of the work conditions for those producing what we might choose to consume.

Now we are getting somewhere. With this knowledge we could have empathy for the workers. We could begin to overcome what is called alienation by starting to understand that each item we consume is really part of a social process rather than some finished independent entity with no history, links, or human dimension.

- We could add knowledge of the byproducts and all outputs of the production processes required to make available what we might choose to consume.

More progress. More connectedness. More qualitative information relevant to our decisions.

- We could add knowledge of the impact that our consumption of items might have on our neighbors and community.

As above.

Next I noted that in each of the above cases, we could encapsulate the added knowledge in the form of a price structure that more accurately incorporates all cost and benefits in the number we are presented, or we could have the information in a more qualitative or descriptive form, or we could have both.

Well, I guess that in my above answers I temporarily cheated by mostly assuming away the inaccurate prices problem. But now let me clarify it. Even the best allocation system is not going to have numbers (prices) which perfectly match real social costs and benefits. At best, they will be a very close representation. But there is an important problem lurking here, even assuming prices reflect all effects.

When something is a little off, a tiny bit, it is generally no cause for alarm. That is the nature of measurement. But, what if error accumulates. That is, suppose a price that deviates inexorably, however little, leads to choices which then cause further distortions in the same direction, and on, and on. Minor errors that arise for whatever reason are multiplied over time. Now you need some kind of corrective for your prices, which will inevitably have errors, to avoid those small errors leading to large problems. And you also need to be sure that the errors are truly random, rather than systematic. (Notice, with markets the errors in prices are systematic, due to not accounting for public and external effects, and so the problem of errors accumulating—Hahnel and I call it snowballing—is acute and also lacks a significant corrective mechanism). Anyhow, the point here is that there is a second purpose for the incorporation of qualitative information into a desirable economic system. First, it reduces alienation and facilitates solidarity (as well as empowerment through knowledge) as noted earlier. But, second, it acts as a corrective to prices alone which are, after all, supposed to be a congealed representation of all qualitative information.

The third focus in this chapter has been how much say should we each have in the final resolution of what we get to fulfill our claims on productive output? Should it be our choice alone? Should others have impact? What context facilitates the preferred balance?

- Do we just get what we say we want, with the sole constraint being that it is consistent with our income?

Since it is consistent with our income, it is equitable. But what if our choices impact on our neighbors? Or what if the workers don't want to expand output of some good we are trying to get a whole lot of? It seems that this issue is like that of information, but at the decision level. It should not be that prices alone are accountable for determining that people's wills are exercised in the right proportions given the effects people endure. The prices are guiding tools ("indicative" is the economic term), but there also ought to be qualitative information to use in these determinations.

- Should the make up of our returns be influenced by people who are affected by how we live our lives, in turn affected by what we consume? And if so, what does this translate to as a guideline? Suppose I want to buy a pet alligator for the back yard. Shouldn't the neighbor have a say in that?

On the one hand, we want a degree of privacy. I don't want to have to ask for permission for everything I consume. On the other hand, my choices can affect the quality of life in my living group or neighborhood. And so what I consume affects others, who therefore should have some level of impact (proportionate, of course) on the outcome.

- What should be the relation between group needs and individual needs in the process of arriving at outcomes?

I don't know that there's a right answer, but it seems to me that you first have to resolve collective needs and consumption, and then in the context of those choices arrive at lower level, smaller group choices, or individual choices. Whether I get skis depends on whether the region I am in chooses to maintain ski lifts, for example.

In the final question I was merely seeking out awareness that there are goods that primarily affect individuals, small groups, larger groups, etc. And so there will need to be mechanisms for arriving at preferences at each relevant level and awareness that there is a logic in trying to deal with the more encompassing consumption first, as it establishes a context for the smaller group and individual choices.

5. Allocation Values

What aims guide our choice of allocation institutions?

"To enjoy the things we ought, and to hate the things we ought has the greatest bearing on excellence of character."

—Aristotle

"His name was George F. Babbitt, and ... he was nimble in the calling of selling houses for more than people could afford to pay."

—Sinclair Lewis

In this chapter we will try to hone our general values into specifics bearing on allocation issues.

ALLOCATION VALUES

THE NEXT TOPIC, THE LAST WE WILL DEAL WITH explicitly under the focus of values, is allocation values. How do we refine our broad values for the economy as a whole into more precise aims vis-à-vis allocation? Well, we do it, presumably, by thinking about what exactly allocation is, and then seeking to understand what kinds of specific aims we want for how we accomplish allocation so that it will further equity, solidarity, self-management, diversity, and efficiency.

So what is allocation?

Suppose we have something we'll call economic activity. We have already seen that it can be production or consumption.

In fact we have seen that production, which has diverse inputs becoming diverse outputs, and consumption, which also has diverse inputs becoming diverse outputs, are in some sense the same. We use the word production when we are concerned about the outputs and the process of their creation. We use the word consumption when we are keying on the inputs. But each act of production also has what we can sensibly call a consumption moment, or aspect. And, likewise, each act of consumption also has what we can call a production moment or aspect.

Now consider the economy as a whole. Over a period of time lots and lots of stuff is taken in, processed, and then distributed to folks and entities (such as groups and institutions) and utilized by them, in turn. Allocation is the name we give to economy activity when we want to focus on the aspect of determining the final lay of the land—what goes where, what is done and not done.

Each act of consumption and production clearly has an allocation moment or aspect. For each act of production/consumption certainly influences this overall outcome for the economy. Yet there are some economic actions that are more allocational, in our sense, than others. For example, the interaction of actors deciding what to buy and sell in a market system or the process of the planning board meeting and proposing inputs and outputs for the steel industry in a centrally planned economy are both primarily allocational, rather than productive or consumptive. Yet these acts are also themselves part and parcel of consumption and production. We choose to feature them, however, when we are talking about the allocation aspect of economic activity.

So, when talking about allocation we are talking about determination of outcomes. Again, consider a society at a moment in time, say January 1 of year 2000. It has a certain condition, and it has certain possibilities. Indeed, imagine some kind of God could come down, take a look around, and then list all possible outcomes for December

31 of that same year in that same society. You have this and that. She has so and so. We have done such and such. Or, alternatively, this other arrangement is the result. And so on, through a nearly infinite list of possibilities. There are different amounts of this and that produced, with different actors, choices about technologies, and distributions of the products (and byproducts) in each different possible societal economic result. Now suppose we look at the same society on December 31 of year 2000. Of all the possibilities, one has eventuated. We can call this the plan for the year 2000. Of course we have found it out after the fact, but, nonetheless, it is a map of what happened, and is, in precisely that sense, an enacted plan, whether or not anyone wrote it out before the fact or not.

So, allocation is the economic process of whittling down from all the conceivable possible outcomes (plans) to the outcome that actually transpires (the enacted plan). What does the whittling? It depends on the economy. Market dynamics might do some of it, or central planners, or both. CEOs of firms may do some of it, or government bureaucrats. Workers might do some of it, as might consumers. So what is the point?

Well, in thinking about allocation, with no biases interfering, what we want to ask is how should the whittling process occur in a good economy? What factors should be taken into account? How should knowledge of these factors be encapsulated and communicated to those who need it? What aims should be sought by those making decisions? And who should be making the choices in the first place, and with what level of impact? Then, if we have aims regarding these matters, we will be able to design institutions to carry out the injunctions.

So, we know our broad values. We know, also, that in thinking about economic inputs and outputs we have much more in mind than just material things. (We also know that we have some aims already in mind for production and consumption, and we of course want allocation to operate consistently with these.) So, as with production and consumption, perhaps we can move toward some clarity about allocation by pursuing various questions concerning it. These might not be quite as easy to even try to answer as those in prior chapters. But nobody said this would be easy all the time. And I have no doubt that those trying to answer are going to get far more out of this than those who just wait around for a few pages for my answers.

• What kinds of decisions do workers (remembering self-management in the workplace) need to be making in the production process?

- What information do workers need to have to make informed, solidaritous, equitable decisions about the options they face?

- Under markets and central planning, what are the answers to the prior two questions, not only for workers, but for other classes too? How do we want things to change?

- What kinds of decisions do consumers need to be making to determine what they want for their share of society's output?

- What kinds of information do consumers need to have at their disposal to make informed, solidaritous, equitable decisions about the options they face?

- Under markets and central planning, what are the answers to the prior two questions? How do we want things to change?

- How can all this needed knowledge be conveyed?

- How is the economic information conveyed in markets and central planning? What do we want to change between this and a good economy?

- What kind of organizational groupings can exist to deal with the fact that some choices are collective? Does it affect information requirements?

- If I need to know what you are wanting and willing to produce, and you need to know what I am wanting and willing to produce, before either of us can make decisions, and if our choices are going to change in light of changes that others make in their choices, and we are all going to participate, how can we possibly arrive at any conclusion?

- What should be the relation between my consumption budget, the amount I am going to work, your budget, the amount you are going to work, and the whole economic product?

- Does the prior question have any answer in a market or centrally planned economy?

- Remembering that we have balanced job complexes, what will therefore be the main determinants of my income, even without knowing the components of my job complex? And is this how we want it to be?

- Should a particular workplace produce a new line of goods or not? What should govern this? What should we weigh off? How can it occur in some social process with the relevant actors having sensible input?

- What is the desirable criteria for determining whether my workplace gets what it wants by way of a new technological innovation? What about your workplace? What about my workplace versus yours? What is the impact of a new technological innovation installed in some part of the economy?

- What should determine the length of the work day? The volume of output for society? How much is set aside for calamities?

- How should the ecology, or future generations, or the requirements of gender decisions be accounted for by a good allocation system?

- What does a plan for the economy need to enunciate? How much detail about what is going to transpire?

- What should be the incentives that encourage people to fulfill their respective roles in the year's plan?

I guess that's enough in the way of questions preparatory to next chapter. One thing critical to this conceptualizing business is obviously thinking up the questions in the first place. If you are trying to develop a theory or model, you need to figure out your concepts, then you need to address the topic by trying to tease out what matters from what is really less consequential. One way to do this is by asking questions and answering them, and working the results into a theory, or vision. Actually, what really happens is more likely that you keep refining your choice of concepts, and your understanding of their interrelations, in light of how you answer the questions that you ask, until you get to a compelling picture. That is what we are doing, anyhow.

So how do you come up with the questions? Well, partly it is just creative and thus hard to give rules for, but partly there is a knack. You try to ask questions that isolate aspects you care about, that differentiate among alternatives, that reveal underlying causes and effects. And you try to be disciplined about it, meaning you try not to jump to answers (which, if spontaneous, may be infected with presuppositions, prejudices, and just downright errors of myth) but to slowly and carefully work out answers paying special attention to using your conceptual toolbox, and to expanding it only when you absolutely need to.

At this point the idea is to think about the above questions in light of the values we have posited and any others you may prefer, and what we have already said about our attitudes to production and consumption (our view of job complexes, remuneration according to effort and sacrifice, and so on), and using the many concepts we've developed.

Answers to Questions

"Any order of phenomena, however complicated, may be studied scientifically provided the rule of proceeding from the simple to the complex is always observed."

—Walras

- What kinds of decisions do workers (remembering self-management in the workplace) need to be making in the production process?

Well, they need to be making those decisions that affect them, in proportion as they are affected by them. So, clearly, they need to be making decisions about the organization of the workplace, the pace of work, and the allocation of responsibilities at a very high level of impact. They need to be making decisions about output level and product characteristics, at a high but not by any means exclusive level of impact. Every choice that must be resolved for each workplace has to be determined by some mechanism that combines the wills of the workers in that unit and the wills of the consumers and the broader public affected by the unit's actions, in the proper proportion.

- What information do workers need to have to make informed, solidaritous, equitable decisions about the options they face?

If I work someplace and have to make choices about how much work I should do or how much product for consumption the plant should produce, I have to know both the true social costs (in required material inputs, in the time of work and the quality of workers' circumstances, in pollution, in effects on workers) and the true social benefits arising from the use the product is put to.

One possibility is that I get this information in some kind of congealed form such as a price that succinctly summarizes all of it.

Another possibility, more humane and informative about real social relationships, but with additional communications requirements and ease of use problems, is that I get this information, or at least access to it when I need it, in all its qualitative glory.

Suppose consumer demand for refrigerators suddenly jumps. Is the only thing I need to know that people say that they want more? No, I need to know why, because I need to know whether the costs associated with choosing to raise my plant's refrigerator output (or my plant's freon output for use by the refrigerator industry) are warranted by the gains that will accrue from people having access to the new fridges. How might I get that information? Perhaps in a changed price that reflects their desire, as well as the added social costs of meeting it. Also, however, my economy might enable me to easily access qualitative data, descriptive accounts, to determine that a bunch of air conditioners made in the past have suddenly punked out, explaining the unusual increase in demand, or that there is a new game that can only be played in a cold room (which might not move me near as much, at least at first take).

> • Under markets and central planning, what are the answers
> to the prior two questions (not only for workers, but for
> other classes too)? And how do we want things to change?

Under markets each worker has the option to choose only whether or not to sell their labor power to their employer, or to try to switch to some other job, or perhaps to fight for better conditions in the current one. Within the workplace, below the coordinator class level, all but low-relevance decisions about production are already taken. Yes, we have to decide how to move our bodies, for example, within the constraint of getting the job done, but that's about it unless we are rebelling against our conditions and therefore operating outside or against the economy's logic.

For the coordinator class, however, the decision process is more complex. On the one hand, subordinate to capital and wanting to keep their jobs at capital's behest, they need to know the implications of each choice for the only thing that matters to capital: bottom line outcomes including short-term profit and longer-term market share and economic power. But from their own perspective, like workers, coordinators also need to decide where they wish to be working and, wherever that might be, they can try to improve their conditions of work, their power at work, and their income, at that site. This generally involves making themselves as indispensable as possible (which is rarely the same as maximizing profits or the dominance of capital) and leads to interesting questions about efficiency and waste from different angles of interest.

As to capitalists, they need to know who to employ to have their workplaces pursue the ends they seek. And they need to know how to extract the obedience and effort they seek. Or, if they are on the site themselves, they need to know the bottom line issues bearing on costs and revenue. Capital and coordinators need to know, therefore, what the public is willing to pay for products, what it costs to hire labor and purchase resources, how to organize work to reduce the power of labor to demand more income or to slow the pace of their efforts, etc.

Note, the information required isn't the implications of consuming the product for people or society (much less the full implications of production decisions for the well-being of workers or the community). These are only a second order concerns, at best, and then only as they affect what really matters, which is profits and the ability to appropriate them.

The price of goods, conveniently for the interests of those dominating the economy, does not represent the full implications of economic choices on everyone affected. Prices instead summarize power relations, not full social costs and benefits, and this is precisely in tune with what dominant classes need to carry out their responsibilities.

Under central planning the workers in plants need to know nothing other than the orders they have to fulfill and the techniques they need to use to do it. The planners may have different needs. Arguably, they need to know the full social costs and benefits of each possible choice, so they can create a socially optimal plan, assuming that is their assignment. In practice, however, they generally need some awareness of overall impact and effects, but will be much more interested in how economic alternatives that they must choose among impact on their own positions in society, particularly their power and their income.

• What kinds of decisions do consumers need to be making to determine what they want for their share of society's output?

How much they want to work. What they want to own.

• What kinds of information do consumers need to have at

their disposal to make informed, solidaritous, equitable
decisions about the options they face?

I can't buy something responsibly without confidence that my choice
is a socially sensible one. I need to know, therefore, the benefits to me,
but also the costs to society and to other individuals of making what I
want available to me. This information could be conveyed by prices—
assuming they represent true social costs and benefits—or by qualitative accounts that convey a textured and revealing picture of just what
goes on in production, allocation, and consumption.

> • Under markets and central planning, what are the answers
> to the prior two questions, not only for workers but for other
> classes too? How do we want things to change?

In markets and central planning there is no way to know anything
about the circumstances of others, nor to account for such information in one's consumption preferences—at least within the norms of
these systems. Thus all that is needed is a price, a budget, and some
information about the purpose and character of products (sort of what
advertising is), where all of these bits of information are, however, not
about costs and benefits, but about power, and are in any event skewed
by power to serve its interests (as in advertising that manipulates rather
than informing, for the obvious reason that the seller's interest is to
sell, not to meet needs or provide means to fulfill real desires).

> • How can all this needed knowledge be conveyed?

Well, one possibility, as already noted, is that it is encapsulated in a
number, a price, which represents a tally of all social costs and benefits.
Another possibility is that the information is conveyed qualitatively,
as accounts of workplace conditions, information about inputs and
outputs, and so on. It may well be, indeed, that we have to use both
information mechanisms. The first has the virtue of brevity and ease
of use in trying to make determinations. For example, we don't know
how much we should opt to consume, to take our share, but not more
than our share. If prices are accurate, our budget tells us this quickly
and lets us operate on the insight easily.

The second approach, qualitative accounts, on the other hand, has
the virtue of empowering us, expanding our awareness, facilitating solidarity and empathy, and—and this proves to be quite important—of
being less subject to unseen biases and therefore of providing a kind of
check on and corrective of digital prices.

- How is economic information conveyed in markets and central planning? What do we want to change between this and a good economy?

In markets there are prices (which convey the available knowledge, which is not, however, a tally of all social costs and benefits but instead a tally of what people are willing to pay and able to charge in light of their bargaining power). There is also advertising, geared to generate a sale, regardless of the actual benefits that would accrue to the user thereby.

In central planning information and motivations can take a variety of forms. Inevitably, however, the wills of planners will predominate and in time skew information (including prices and descriptive accounts) in ways corresponding with their view of the world, and their interests within the economy. More, in central planning the information is not available for people below the top to make decisions, but for people to implement decisions made by others.

Presumably, in a good economy we want information to provide a full accounting of implications of economic actions, consistent with decision making by those affected and the insight that nobody would want to produce or sell anything that wasn't going to benefit consumers—why waste one's time in such a ludicrous or even counterproductive pursuit?

- What kind of organizational groupings can exist to deal with the fact that some choices are collective? Does it affect information requirements?

We can have units that operate collectively in their decision making. In workplaces this can be anything from a work group or team to a workplace or industry wide council. Regarding consumption, this can include living groups, living areas, neighborhoods, and counties beyond the level of the individual.

- If I need to know what you are wanting and willing to produce, and you need to know what I am wanting and willing to produce, before either of us can make decisions, and if our choices are going to change in light of changes that others make in their choices, and we are all going to participate, how can we possibly arrive at any conclusion?

It seems to follow that we have to have a kind of self-conscious negotiating process in which there is a steady accrual of information about desires and preferences, all providing a context for people to make known their choices, and to in turn moderate them in light of the choices other people opt for, until there is a workable outcome. The other three options are each inconsistent with one or more of our guiding values of equity, self-management, solidarity, diversity, and efficiency. They are a kind of dynamic exchange in which power or competition acts to constrain outcomes down to final choices (markets), or a top down determination of choices (central planning), or a (well-motivated but ultimately counter-productive) decentralization of economic scale so extreme that all decisions are made on the spot, by all concerned and affected, because there is little division of labor or need for complex allocation at all.

- What should be the relation between my consumption budget, the amount I am going to work, your budget, the amount you are going to work, and the whole economic product?

If I am working at a balanced job complex, the length of my work time at this complex is a measure of my effort and sacrifice. With equity, what I get for that average exercise is an average income. With these equilibrations, the value of my consumption budget should match the value of yours, and of everyone else's. The only variation would be due to my working overtime, or my taking extra time off, etc. But this means that my proposal for how much I want to work is also, implicitly, a statement about the total social product and about how much I (and everyone else) will be budgeted to consume.

- Does the prior question have any answer in a market or centrally planned economy?

Not really. There is no regular relation, other than as mediated through bargaining power in the market economy, between consumption preferences and work outlays in markets. And in the planned economy, it depends on the norms of distribution that are employed and the class biases of planners.

- Remembering that we have balanced job complexes, what will therefore be the main determinants of my income, even without knowing the components of my job complex? And is this how we want it to be?

How long do I work? The idea is simple. Imagine we all do precisely the same task. Then what is the measure of effort and sacrifice? Clearly it is duration. Now, supposing that we all do different things, if their overall qualitative impact on our quality of life and empowerment are equal, duration is still the right measure. And I think this is fine. It is quite consistent with everything we have postulated so far as guiding values.

- Should a particular workplace produce a new line of goods or not? What should govern this? What should we weigh off in deciding? How can it occur in some social process with the relevant actors having sensible input?

Well, what will be the costs of beginning this new line? And what will be the benefits? We are going to need some resources (which could go to other ends instead). There may be some pollution. Producing the new line could be onerous work. But if we undertake the innovation we will have this new product people will benefit from. So the question is, does the benefit out weigh the cost so that on balance the investment is a good idea compared to other possible uses of our time, resources, and tools. As to how the decision can be reached by real people in real time, my answer on that will have to wait until coming discussions.

- What is the desirable criteria for determining whether my workplace gets what it wants by way of a new technological innovation? What about your workplace? What about my workplace versus yours? What is the impact of a new technological innovation installed in some part of the economy?

This question is pretty interesting, I think. Suppose I work in a plant that produces refrigerators, and you work in a publishing house. By this time we hopefully realize that if the values implemented in our economy are those we have highlighted so far in our discussions, in my plant and in yours there are going to be balanced job complexes. Moreover, if in your publishing house the average job complex is more desirable than the societal average (which is pretty likely) and in my refrigerator factory it is less desirable, then I will get to work some hours outside of my factory at a nice and empowering set of tasks, and you will have to work some hours outside your publishing house, balancing off its quality job offerings with some onerous tasks elsewhere.

Now suppose someone in my factory comes up with an idea for changing the assembly line to make the work more desirable. And someone in your publishing house also comes up with an innovative idea, having to do with improving your phone system that would improve conditions for editorial work. Which investment should be a higher priority to undertake—from a social perspective? What about from your perspective and mine?

Well, from society's viewpoint we prefer to undertake the innovation that will have the larger positive effect on work roles and outputs compared to its cost. But—and this is the interesting thing—whereas in a market or a centrally planned economy you would prefer that the innovation in your workplace be enacted and I would prefer that the innovation in my refrigerator plant be enacted, regardless of their relative merits, in a parecon we would each prefer that whichever of the two innovations would have the larger positive effect be enacted. I find this to be a remarkably robust and alluring attribute of parecon. That is, in parecon over time the only impact that ultimately affects us is not proximity to an innovation, but any innovation's implications for the overall average societal job complex (if the complex gets better, everyone gets a better job and if average societal job complex gets worse everyone gets a worse one, regardless of where the innovation occurs and of where people work); or the overall social product (if it gets larger we get a bigger consumer budget, if it gets smaller we get a smaller consumer budget, again regardless of where we live or work). Therefore, with this system we inevitably benefit most from what everyone benefits most from, and vice versa. Something to think about. We innovate in the coal mine. How long does it take for the innovation's positive effects to be averaged out so that everyone everywhere has the same gain in their lives due to it? What are the implications of our choices about how long this averaging should take? What is the rhetoric in a market economy about innovations, and what is the reality?

> • What should determine the length of the work day? The
> volume of output for society? How much is set aside for
> calamities?

The length of the work day should be determined by how much leisure people want versus how large a consumption budget they want, assuming attention to all other social costs and benefits. The size and composition of the social product should be shaped by people's preferences for consumption versus their desires to have time to enjoy it, again assuming attention to all other social costs and benefits. How much to set aside for calamities should be determined by good predications as to their likely impact.

What about under markets? Well, in that case the allocation system itself creates a drive for growth that transcends the will of any actors. More, a set of actors given dominant power over outcomes is also given an interest in growth. As a result, in a market system the link between the amount of output desired and the amount of leisure desired is sundered for most people. We have to work our heads off so we want as much as we can have.

There is a similar, but weaker tendency in a centrally planned economy, where certain kinds of innovations and grandiose scale of operations help solidify and enlarge the claims on power of the dominant coordinator class.

About calamities, here is something to think about. What should be the locus of decision making, of payment, and of receipt of payment when there are accidents, grave illnesses, and so on? What is the value being upheld?

- How should the ecology, or future generations, or the requirements of gender decisions be accounted for by a good allocation system?

These, it seems to me, are to be accounted however people choose politically to have them accounted for. That is, they are not intrinsically economic questions, but, in the first place, questions whose answers depend on implementation of cultural structures and gender roles beyond the underlying bounds of economic rationality, though affecting it. There could be ecological norms that must be abided. There could be rules about the volume of output that has to be devoted to investment for betterment of life in the future. There could be rules about gender balance. And so on. We thus want an allocation system that is not only capable of operating sensibly economically, but that is able to do so even while abiding such extra economic injunctions deriving elsewhere in society—just as we want kinship relations, community relations, a polity that are able to function compatibly with the dictates and requirements of our envisioned economy. This degree of flexibility exists, we will see, for parecon. It can also arguably exist for central planning. It does not and cannot exist, however, for markets. Staunch right-wing defenders of markets are right about this. That is, if we claim to want markets because of various virtues we find in them, we are inconsistent when we impose constraints upon their operations. Why? Because the arguments that convinced us markets have certain virtues (which are wrong in any event) lose all their force (even in the eyes of marketeers) once we interfere, even minimally, in market operations.

- What does a plan for the economy need to enunciate? How much detail about what is going to transpire?

This is a bit tricky, I think, and perhaps a little premature. The idea is simple, and then there are just a bunch of statistical "tricks" and other such things that ease the task and figuring out what these "tricks" might be is the key to answering this question.

You want a set of aims for everyone in the economy. Thus, you need to know people's and group's consumption choices, and what each workplace is to produce, by what means, with what inputs and outputs. But in needing to know what everybody is going to consume, how much detail do we need? Can we extrapolate the details, just from knowing certain gross figures and certain reliable things about people, or our population in particular? Thus can we go from number of shirts wanted, to numbers of each size shirt, or type shirt, so closely that we only need the first piece of data to arrive at all the conclusions? What about knowing about nuts, as compared to surveying detailed preferences for all kinds of nuts? Is the former enough to deduce the latter? And so on. Do we each need to predict the likelihood that we will need medicines? Or meet new people or have children unexpectedly? Do we have to predict which nights during the year we are going to want to go out for dinner? Or what will be the amount of food we wish to buy day by day or week by week, for the whole year? Or can all these things be accounted for in a gross and average way by the system, based on extrapolations from broader stated preference of individuals, plus knowledge from past experiences, and so on?

Think about what the workers in a factory creating some product need to know, and what the planning process needs to discern for them to be able to have that required information.

- What should be the incentives that encourage people to fulfill their respective roles in the year's plan?

Well, given our values, it seems like this should be a degree of material incentive—that is, access to a fair share of the social product—and a degree of social and personal incentive, that is, the respect or even the admiration of one's work mates. For this type of incentive system to work—a far cry from the desire to be rich or to avoid poverty—it must be that all alternative and contrary ways of orienting one's priorities are considerably worse. There are, that is, two sides to incentives: Rewarding desirable behavior, and making undesirable behavior unattractive or worthless.

Thus, for example, we can reward effort and sacrifice, both materially and with respect, and we can reward creativity and accomplishment, with respect and emotional responses, and we can structure outcomes so that behavior like shirking, or stealing, or trying to disproportionately influence outcomes yields no gains and only exacts losses for the perpetrator.

- In light of all the above, and our overarching values, and the aims we have already espoused for production and consumption, what do you think ought to be our aims for a desirable allocation system? When all is said and done, what should delimit options down to outcomes?

This question harks back to the description of allocation at the outset of the chapter, and I would like to recontextualize it, to hammer home some of the insights. We have, at the outset of any economic period, an almost infinite array of possible outcomes we might choose for our economy. This great diversity doesn't mean all economies offer up all possible outcomes. This is quite false. For example, class-divided economies don't offer classless outcomes. Economies based on wage slavery don't offer unalienated outcomes. And so on.

But any economy offers countless possible outcomes, even within the limitations of abiding its biases and reproducing its central features. Now, suppose we focus our attention on the various processes that delimit from the immense set of possible outcomes the actual set of outcomes that do in fact transpire. We can call the factors that induce this narrowing of options all the way to a final choice, the *economic processor*. We can also, however, note that it doesn't happen in one immense swoop. Even in the most dictatorial centrally planned economy, there are many facets that influence the narrowing from all possibilities down to one enacted choice—the allocation process, including the operation of many economic processors. Suppose we go back even further. We start out with all the outcomes that are possible given the laws of physics. Then there is, first, a processing of this set of options down by the fact that we have a certain level of technology, certain economic institutions and roles, etc. (This is of course exceptionally important for evaluating alternative economies—that is, they may have different implications for what is possible for production and consumption.)

Anyhow, within a good economy, the upshot of the answers above and of our discussion thus far, I think, is that what we want is that the processor be to the greatest extent possible, the population, pure and simple. The allocation system should manifest people's will on outcomes in proportion as they are affected by those outcomes. It is human need and desire and potential, mediated so that everyone has a fair and proportionate say, that should take society from the almost infinite set of economic possibilities for the year, to what it actually does. And, moreover, the economy's institutions should not delimit the overall possibility set in any way that limits the extent to which we can attain equity, self-management, solidarity, diversity, or efficiency.

6. Production Institutions

Exploring decisions, councils, and job complexes

"Why should workers agree to be slaves in a basically authoritarian structure? They should have control over it themselves. Why shouldn't communities have a dominant voice in running the institutions that affect their lives?"

—Noam Chomsky

"Now, as to occupations, we shall clearly not be able to have the same division of labor as now: vicarious servanting, sewer emptying, butchering, letter carrying, boot-blacking, hair dressing, and the rest of it will have to come to an end ... we shan't put a pattern on a cloth or a twiddle on a jug-handle to sell it, but to make it prettier and to amuse ourselves and others."

—William Morris

We have now completed half of this book. In this chapter, 6, I would like to begin by briefly summarizing some of the ground we have already covered. Then we will move on to the institutional section of our undertaking, including five more chapters, by dealing first with production institutions.

SUMMARY RESULTS OF THE FIRST HALF OF OUR STUDY

LEAVING OUT SOME OF THE DETAILS, so far we have covered the following:

1. A methodology for creating useful vision.

Define our domain of concern. Determine its main component elements. Determine what it is, in broad value terms, that we want to achieve with our vision for this domain. Examine in more detail the main component features, and determine what we want for each of them, broadly speaking. Implement our aims in institutional designs and structures for the component features. Be sure the components that we envision fit together. Be sure the whole vision for our domain fits with the rest of the domains of society. Move on to issues of implementation, refinement, and so on.

2. Clarification of what the economic domain is.

We have highlighted production, consumption, and allocation, and we have clarified what each embodies and involves in terms of types of roles, processes, information, decisions, inputs and outputs, and what their relations to one another are. Our results have been about 180 degrees off from what is typically thought about economics, even by most radicals.

3. Situating our efforts vis-à-vis various types of economies.

We have created a typology of economies and evaluated those we know about in light of their component features, class structure, etc., and the implications of these for human well-being and development. Again, our views have been at odds with generally accepted views, mainstream and radical as well.

4. A clarification of our goals broadly, and for each of the main parts of the economy.

We have settled on four primary guiding values (some of you may have some more you are employing), and we have used these and our clarification of what economics is about, to elaborate more detailed goals for each of the main aspects of any economy, its production, consumption, and allocation institutions. Again, all this is more or less unique to us and in large part contrary to views held by other economists.

Now we are ready to try to actually design some institutional features, first for production, then for consumption, and then for allocation.

PRODUCTION INSTITUTIONS

"The understandings of the greater part of men are necessarily formed by their ordinary employments ... the man whose life is spent in performing a few simple operations, of which the effects too are, perhaps, always the same, or very nearly the same, has no occasion to exert his understanding ... and generally becomes as stupid and ignorant as it is possible for a human creature to be ... But in every improved and civilized society this is the state into which the laboring poor, that is, the great body of people, must necessarily fall, unless government takes pains to prevent it."

—Adam Smith

We finally have reached the stage of trying to design and describe institutional structures that fulfill our aims. Think of a workplace. It could be modest, say ten or fifteen people, or it could be huge, say 1,000 or even 5,000 people. Perhaps a little production unit, or a major university or hospital or assembly operation. Within this place, how do we want decisions to be made? And what organizational forms will we employ to facilitate our preferred decision-making schemes?

DECISIONS

Suppose we think of the workplace as a gigantic process, with inputs and outputs, of course. What are the decisions? Well, what will be produced, by what means, at what pace, with what technologies? What will be the jobs and who will fill them? During each day, how will we get our work done? What will I do, what will you do, how will we mesh our efforts successfully with each other and with others throughout the workplace?

Some of the decisions are interactive with the rest of the economy—they are part and parcel of the broad level of allocation. Some, are more a matter of implementation, organizing the workday given its broad aims. We all know from experience these latter types of decision, and we can easily conceive of the former types, though few of us have probably ever been involved in making any of them.

(If you think in terms of the processor idea—that is, a set of institutions and processes narrowing down possibilities to final choices—regarding allocation, you can see that we are on a particular part of the continuum.)

Now any workplace has some processes and associated decisions that involve many people very interactively and mutually dependently—for example, how much product, what new technology or social organization? And each workplace has some processes and decisions that involve a smaller array of people most directly—for example how should the personnel department or the promotion department organize to accomplish its responsibilities—with the determinations usually dependent on prior higher level choices as well. And some decisions that are narrower still—can I trade responsibilities with you today, what order am I going to do my tasks in this morning—that are, however, limited by a whole array of prior, more encompassing decisions. We also know the general menu of decision making methodologies we can employ, I think.

1. We can have direct face to face debate followed by votes with various rules for determining outcome (such as authoritative decisions, one person, one vote, majority rules, you need two-thirds, etc.).

2. We can have delegation of authority, either by permanent appointment, or recallable representatives, or rotated "office holders."

3. Individuals can be left to decide whatever they want, with differences mediated after the fact.

4. Bosses can be the deciders and the rest followers.

5. Everything can be determined at an overarching level, or decisions can be taken at many levels.

And so the question arises, from among all that is possible, what do we want? What ways of making decisions about the workplace best implement our values: equity, diversity, solidarity, and participatory self-management? Or any others that you may wish to pose as more relevant or more important? And is there only one right answer to this question? Here are some thought questions to pursue:

• What is economic democracy in the workplace and why do

we want it?

- Is there any difference between workplace and polity that justifies a different decision making attitude regarding each?

- What is the difference between utilizing expertise and employing hierarchy regarding workplace decisions and what attitude do you have to each?

- How should decisions over global workplace issues be settled?

- What about implementation decisions concerning the work of a team or other group?

- What about how you do your work at your work station, or desk, or assembly site, or whatever?

- What would be the arguments against what you have proposed, offered by capitalists, offered by coordinators (managers), offered by some workers?

- And how do you refute these arguments?

- Suppose you have one person, one vote, majority rule, and full opportunity for discussion. Do you thereby automatically have desirable democracy and participation?

- If you have a formally desirable structure, might you still have, in practice, undemocratic dynamics? Why? What could be done about it?

- How much can we sensibly ask from our institutional choices?

- What other questions would be useful to consider regarding institutional choices for workplace decision-making structures?

Councils and Job Complexes

In implementing our values and aims in the workplace, so far we have the idea of decision-making by consensus and or diverse vote-level requirements, sometimes with all involved actors voting, sometimes by representative, all done at various natural levels of involvement— the whole workplace council, divisional or section councils, project groups and work teams, and individuals. And we have the overriding proviso that this structure needs to not only be formally democratic in what people are allowed to do—but that the actors engaged in the interactions also have to be prepared to use the possibilities available to them. Thus they must all have background, education, work experience and knowledge sufficient for them to use their formal rights to speak, judge, and vote.

To accomplish this latter aim clearly has implications for schooling and for distribution of information and resources generally. We can't have a sector of society with tremendous access to information at home and others with little, nor a sector with the time and freedom and energy to use such access, and another sector too exhausted to ever take advantage of it. And we certainly can't have a large part of the population educated at school in ways that destroy initiative and deaden potentials, preparing people, against their capacities and inclinations, to endure boredom and embrace passivity, while a much smaller sector is taught to feel that it not only has the right and the wisdom to decide all for itself and for others, but is also given the tools and confidence that give this arrogance a high degree of accuracy.

But, this is not the end of the implications. Much of our time is spent on the job. And much of the foundation for on-the-job participation is on-the-job empowerment or disempowerment. If we divide up work so that some people have job circumstances that do nothing to promote skills and talents and to convey knowledge requisite to decision making, and that instead tend to curtail or totally prevent access to these, or that even destroy such inclinations and possibilities, then these people will not participate much in decision making regardless of formal rights to do so.

And, similarly, if some people have work situations and responsibilities that give them markedly more knowledge and skill and talents and energy for decision making, rather than squander this asset, it is likely that their wills will in almost all instances translate into the will of the whole workplace disproportionately to their numbers or to the degree that outcomes affect them. The above is a powerful reason not to divide work into homogenous job complexes, each of which is of different empowerment impact than the rest. To implement this type job hierarchy is, in the first place, to violate our self-management values, and in the second place it is to produce class divisions, which in turn enhance differentials not only of power, but also of circumstance and income.

A second reason to avoid defining jobs in a hierarchical manner is that it is unjust. There is no moral excuse for having some people occupy less fulfilling work circumstances than others. So what is the solution?

Well, we have argued that it is creation of balanced job complexes, one of the central innovations of the economic vision called parecon. (Or, perhaps you may think of an alternative approach to meeting all these requirements, in response to this chapter, or will raise new objections to the aims themselves.) And so at this point the issue becomes, what are balanced job complexes, how are they established, how do they change over time, how does a person wind up doing one or another, and what are the negative implications of having them, if any.

For purposes of the following questions, I hope readers will think seriously about the issues at hand, in the abstract and also considering your own work experiences. Balanced job complexes means there is no such thing as a traditional secretary, though there are secretarial tasks divided into job complexes along with other tasks. There is no such thing as a janitor. There is a division of labor, far more self-consciously crafted to fulfill values and aims than now, including productivity and efficiency norms, and this division does not allow for inequitable distributions of tasks.

Few if any of us, I suspect, work at what is an average job complex for our workplace much less for the economy as a whole. Indeed, few progressive and left projects enact these norms, mostly incorporating instead structures virtually indistinguishable from those of the companies and corporations they oppose. Here are some questions to help push forward the discussion.

- What is a balanced job complex? What are the arguments for having them? What arguments can you raise against having them?

- What is the refutation of arguments against balancing job complexes, and which way do you lean?

- How would your job change if your work institution were to balance job complexes internally?

- How do you think your job would change if complexes were then also balanced across all workplaces, with the economy as it is?

- What would be the effect of introducing balanced job complexes into your workplace, now? What about as part of a national program that included, for example, retraining?

- What would be the implication of having balanced job complexes in your workplace for the implementation of new technologies and other innovations?

- What is the relationship between having balanced job complexes in a good economy, and the process of deciding on investments or new technologies.

- Does having balanced job complexes oppress anyone, or reduce the well-being of anyone, as compared to having more traditional job arrangements?

- If you like the idea of job complexes, how would you reply to someone saying that they are unfair to very brilliant people, or impose too much responsibility on many people who won't want it?

- Do you have any idea at all what the organizational structure is and internal values are of political projects and institutions that you relate to or support? Why do you think you don't, assuming that is the case?

- If you find the idea of balanced job complexes righteous and valid, or at least plausibly so, I wonder if you could hazard a guess as to why they are not a widely discussed programmatic aim among leftists?

Answers to Questions

"We pass the word around; we ponder how the case is put by different people; we read the poetry; we meditate over the literature; we play the music; we change our minds; we reach an understanding. Society evolves this way, not by shouting each other down, but by the unique capacity of unique, individual human beings to comprehend each other."

—Lewis Thomas

- What is economic democracy in the workplace and why do we want it?

At a minimum economic democracy would be something like one person, one vote on all policy questions, and some form of self-regulation with oversight on everything else. But given our values, economic democracy is something a little more subtle. That is, each worker should have a say in workplace decisions more or less in proportion as he or she is affected by those decisions. How I conduct myself when sweeping, say, or when writing something, is going to affect others mostly in terms of whether I get the task done, unless I want to sing while I work, or something like that, and it bothers others. So, generally, but for exceptional disturbing choices, I decide how to carry out my personal responsibilities myself, within the bounds of fulfilling my responsibilities. It is autocratic, I suppose, but acceptably so.

Likewise, if I work in a small team, we decide our internal operations, again within the bounds of fulfilling our team assignments. That is, within the bounds set by our overarching responsibilities, and the constraint that we not disrupt others' activities, we have essentially dictatorial say over our group. But, we do not have a dictator, but instead divide up the decision-making responsibilities within our team democratically. There are, of course, many ways this could be done.

The additional constraint, in both cases—me alone and me in a team—is that our choices have to be within the broad value norms that guide the economy, and they have to be in tune with not having deleterious affects on others (since, if they do, those others will gain a say and intervene).

So what do we have? It seems that workplace democracy implies having layers of decision-making influence including individuals, teams, work groups, maybe sections of the work place or divisions, the whole workplace, and then more broadly, the industry. Each of these layers or levels would operate in context of decisions at a higher level and in respect of the implications for lower levels. We can call the larger units councils, the smaller ones teams and individuals.

> • Is there any difference between workplace and polity that
> justifies a different decision making attitude regarding each?

I don't see one, other than the exigencies of the particular types of decision.

> • What is the difference between utilizing expertise and
> employing hierarchy regarding workplace decisions and
> what attitude do you have to each?

The difference is that in one case we are doing something productive with no necessary deleterious moral impact (taking account of specialized knowledge or skill) and in the other case we are doing something often not productive and in any event always engendering deleterious effects (using fixed hierarchies).

There is a difference between consulting an expert, or having an expert examine circumstances and propose options with accompanying assessments of implications, and letting the expert make decisions. I need someone to tell me about the implications of using lead paint. But I can decide for or against using it, based on that special information. Same for nuclear power. Same for most anything. So in a workplace there will frequently be cause for reports and commentary from people with special knowledge or who have specially investigated a question, but then the decision can be taken in light of that information, by all affected.

Indeed, the principle of paying attention to expert knowledge leads inexorably away from depending on experts for decision-making. In fact, since I am the world's foremost expert on my preferences, you on yours, and since a decision is supposed to account for our preferences proportionately, by the criteria of paying attention to expert knowledge when it is relevant, we must be involved proportionately in decisions that need to account for our preferences.

• How should decisions over global workplace issues be settled?

The word "global" here implies to me that these are the decisions that affect the whole workplace, and everyone in it. I should think these would generally be concerns about broad policy, to be decided by a vote (with, perhaps, some special requirements about what percentage is necessary for a victory) of the whole workplace council.

Could some workplaces, or all of them, sometimes incorporate delegation of decision-making about some matters? Yes, I don't see why not, if it is consistent with guiding values and efficient or otherwise desirable to take this approach.

• What about implementation of decisions concerning the work of a team or other group?

Unless some choice might have impact on others and beyond the obvious issue of getting their job done, I should think this would be a matter for the group or team in question.

• What about how you do your work at your work station, or desk, or assembly site, or whatever?

Again, save for the impact that some strange choices might have on others, it would seem that this decision generally rests with me. I might need to coordinate with my work mates in some cases, of course, but generally my personal work choices within the norms and goals of my job complex, mostly affect me.

- What would be the arguments against what you have proposed, offered by capitalists, offered by coordinators (managers), offered by some workers?

I don't want to answer this too fully, as we will deal with these matters more later. But I can imagine critics saying: people don't have the ability for this level of involvement; teaching people would be too expensive and draining; people don't want this level of involvement and democracy; it would be inefficient, lacking the order of more command-based models; and the meetings would take too long. Indeed these points have all been raised publicly, in reviews of parecon presentations, and will be addressed in chapter 10.

- And how do you refute these arguments?

I think this will emerge in coming sessions—but in every case there are two issues: is what we are seeking consistent with our guiding values, and is the critique in fact of those values (in which case we defend or jettison them), or are the values accepted and the criticism is that our choice of elaborating balanced job complexes is not in accord with them (in which case we discuss the logic and implications of job structures and their implementation).

- Suppose you have one person, one vote, and majority rule. Plus full opportunity for discussion. Do you thereby automatically have desirable democracy and participation?

No. Because I only have an equal say over my own circumstances as you and everyone else in the workplace, even if we are talking about just how I will organize my tasks over the course of my work day, and even if the choice has no effect on anyone but me. The decision making influence is off, and also it makes no sense to discuss such matters at length. I don't want to hear anyone else's view, save as a kind of advisory or consultation that I may seek, much less do I want to have to debate other people about when I get to go to the water fountain, or what order I do my tasks in, unless it affects them or is thought to violate some socially agreed norms.

- If you have a formally desirable structure, might you still have, in practice, undemocratic dynamics? Why? What could be done about it?

By all means. Suppose we have one person, one vote for broad encompassing policy decisions that affect everyone more or less equally—a perfectly reasonable choice. But suppose when we get together to have our session discussing these matters a very few people have the information needed to even have an opinion, and also have the skills and disposition required for developing and arguing for an agenda, and the rest of us don't know anything we aren't told, and moreover have neither the disposition nor the skills to create or evaluate opposed agendas. And suppose the division of the whole group into these sectors always comes out the same, with the same people in respective positions.

In the discussion we can say without much doubt that the few who have knowledge and skills and disposition to adjudicate, create options, evaluate them, and make decisions, will dominate. In every vote, as they vote, so too will the rest of us. The democracy is only formal because underneath it there is a very real hierarchy of influence and power. Of course, such a hierarchy will soon act to entrench and reward itself, and to institutionalize the imbalance of power even more forcefully.

It seems the only thing we can do to ward off this type of compromise of our decision—making structures is to make sure that by both schooling and on-the-job effects everyone is empowered sufficiently so that the formal democracy inevitably becomes actualized in a truly participatory framework. We must avoid having jobs whose character is such that people in different jobs are markedly differently empowered by them.

- How much can we sensibly ask from our institutional choices?

Quite a bit, I think. We can demand that they not impose modes of behavior, or calculation, or interaction, or divisions of power or status or means, contrary to the values we hold. And then we can go a step further and demand that they not only function consistently with those values and not subvert them, but that working within our chosen institutions actually promotes personality, awareness, skills, knowledge, and interests, that facilitate pursuit of those values.

- What is a balanced job complex? What are the arguments for having them? What arguments can you raise against having them?

A balanced job complex (BJC) is a combination of tasks such that the overall quality of work and overall empowerment characteristics of the total job are equilibrated to those of other jobs. There is one proviso which we haven't yet spoken much about. If it is OK with work mates, if it fits the production requirements of one's firm, and so on, one can trade a bit (either working longer with more income, or less long with less income, or perhaps picking up some extra onerous work again, to earn extra income, while someone else is doing somewhat less of the onerous work, earning somewhat less income). Trades are not permitted that disrupt equilibration of empowerment effects. Thus, with balanced job complexes empowerment is balanced among job assignments throughout the economy. Quality of work is balanced, with the possibility of deviations up or down from the average, offset by countervailing income changes.

The arguments in favor of BJCs are that they are the best possible choice of how to combine tasks into jobs if we are concerned that there be an equitable allocation of desirable and not-so-desirable and downright undesirable work effects (conditions plus income), and an equitable allocation of empowerment implications of jobs for workers to allow and promote truly democratic decision-making by all.

The most frequently raised arguments against BJCs are: they oppress the highly knowledgeable or highly skilled by forcing them to spend some time in mundane work; they misutilize training and skills by having people waste these attributes by working at tasks that don't need their accumulated ability and training; they require people to struggle to work at a level they are not able to, demanding of people participation and involvement beyond their ken; they require too much schooling for too many people; they are hard to design and to continually update.

> • What is the refutation of arguments against balancing job
> complexes, and which way do you lean?

I think I will answer these with my unabashed unalloyed sentiments ...

> • BJCs oppress the highly knowledgeable or highly skilled by
> forcing them to spend some time in mundane work.

Tough.

That is to say, any society has a certain amount of onerous, dangerous, tedious, or otherwise not preferred work. Now why the hell should this be disproportionately done by some people while others enjoy better work conditions?

Do we oppress a slave owner by changing to a situation in which owning slaves is no longer permitted? We take away an advantage and an option, to be sure. But to call this oppression reveals much.

Do we oppress a set of people previously able to work at only desirable tasks if we establish the norm that everyone has to do their fair share of onerous tasks? We take away an advantage and an option, to be sure. Doesn't calling this oppression reveal much?

It is not oppressive, in short, that a person has to do their fair share. It is oppressive, instead, whenever any person must do a disproportionately great share of something undesirable so that another person can do less than a fair share.

The argument that the person currently avoiding these job tasks (by virtue of being a doctor, lawyer, or holding some other coordinator role, or perhaps by being a top level professional athlete) is being oppressed by having their advantages taken back to improve the situation of those who truly have been oppressed, is rubbish. It wouldn't be worthy of discussion, it is so obviously grotesque in its assumptions, but for the fact that we live in a society in which the grotesque has become enshrined as common sense gospel.

There will be a time in the future when this argument about BJCs will appear to people just as horrid as arguments that abolition oppressed slave owners appears to us now.

- BJCs misutilize great training and skills by having people with these wasting their time working at tasks that don't need all this training and talent.

First off, once everybody has training, there is no way to avoid that trained people will be sometimes doing things that do not require their learned skills, or full talents. So, the real question becomes, in some sense, do we have everyone develop, or do we develop only enough people so that no resources are spent on development that does not, in turn, get used at full capacity in production.

Put this way, it makes sense to curtail education and training to the minimum level needed to complete desired production: if education and training is onerous and not pleasant in its own right; and if education and training have no benefits that transcend the implications for economic output (or, in some economies, profit). The underlying assumptions necessary for the complaint to even register as remotely sensible are therefore, to me, truly disgusting.

As a parallel, suppose someone said society should only feed people the amount necessary for them to work at the rate that their productive role in society (established by some élite, no less) requires (which, was, indeed, the notion predominant among capitalists before considerable labor struggle forced a different approach). With the exception of those at the top, the assumption is that people work, eat, and do some other irrelevant nonsense of no account, and should get no more from society than is needed to carry out those two critical functions.

But that is only one problem with the complaint. Another reply might be: Yeah, sure. Causing, say, 20 percent of the population to pick up its fair share of onerous and non-empowering work may perhaps utilize their stored up skills, training, and talents less than if we didn't require that onerous work of them assumes that the people in question are using their skills for full workdays and work weeks before such a change, and also ignores the extent to which these people are currently using these stored traits in socially useless or destructive ways merely maintaining their advantages.

But, give them the claim. Assume that these folks, if we don't have BJCs, will do only socially valuable work and will do it every hour and day they work, with no stretches of idleness, long lunches, or golf trips. What about the other 80 percent of the population? Those who would be freed to develop their capacities and abilities and to put them to use if the top twenty percent did their fair share of onerous and not empowering work? To take this objection to BJCs as a serious argument we have to believe that each person in the twenty percent will be, on average, four times more productive than each person in the eighty percent, plus additional to make up for use of the twenty percent enforcing their own dominance. It is utter nonsense and to even think it, it seems to me, again reveals underlying attitudes that are not too pretty, and that we ought to be uncovering and removing from our consciousness.

But suppose for a minute that the distribution of potentials among people, the costs of training, and the nature of contemporary job tasks made the claim valid. Say the twenty percent would be six times more productive per hour, on average, than the eighty percent, even with each constituency fully developing its skills and capacities. Even with this outrageous assumption, for a person with an iota of moral sensibility, it wouldn't matter. Because attaining classlessness, equity, solidarity, etc., so much offsets in worth any conceivable difference in productivity (were such a productivity difference to actually exist in the first place). So, again, the complaint reflects not only a jaundiced view about what people in different constituencies can and can't do, even under ideal circumstances, it also reflects a jaundiced view of what matters in life, it seems to me.

Finally, the real productivity effect of instituting BCJs would be an immense gain especially if we are talking about the utilization of productive possibilities for creating things that are actually of social value.

- BJCs require people to struggle to work at a level they are not able to, demanding of people participation and involvement beyond their ken.

I always answer this complaint patiently and without rancor, because I suppose I think that is civil and tactically right if the goal is to actually communicate and not affront people into resistance, but to be out front about my real feelings, which is what I am trying to do in this answer, I find this complaint almost too repulsive to reply to. Yeah, sure. Most people are genetically incapable of the immense degree of genius associated with making decisions about economic matters, exercising self-management, assessing diverse information and evidence, in a field of their choosing, in a congenial environment. Who would this be? This person who would be crushed by the weight of having their talents and skills nourished and then having to actually take responsibility for their own life?

The same person who is a master of NBA strategy and statistics on the weekend even though now having to spend fifty hours a week on a mind-deadening assembly line, perhaps? Or the doctor or lawyer who despite immense education and huge tracts of time for reading, is self-deceptive and ignorant enough to believe that the U.S. was in Vietnam to free the Vietnamese to live a better life?

The housewife now raising three kids and dealing with low-budget shopping and the juggling of countless decisions and demands, while fending off all sorts of patriarchal incursions and attacks on her dignity and intelligence, or the plant manager or engineer who has had endless years of schooling and who still has ample time for study but who nonetheless thinks blacks are inferior or that technology is chosen on purely objective productivity grounds?

And so on.

You know, a rather more accurate take on the situation, I think, is that in our society, most often, garbage rises ... and so the real question is whether those now enjoying great advantages could ever manage to undo their socialization and lunatic value structures and belief systems to function in a humane and responsible fashion. I think yes, but this is at least a plausible concern.

• BJCs require too much schooling for too many people.

This is another good one. We might reply by asking, what is the alternative approach that this person must prefer? We have only so many educational resources in any society. What should we do with them? Suppose we use the criteria that we ought to utilize them where they will have the largest impact on output, a criteria that this critic will employ whenever it suits him or her. If the product is schooling, meaning increased levels of competence and knowledge, then surely with the exception of pathological cases, to use the resources to advance those who have least ability to teach themselves, or least prior learning, would be optimal.

Second, how can one even consider the idea that society ought to give people less schooling or that it is educating too many people?

In other words, under the surface all these types of objections strike me in more or less the same way that I imagine analogous questions of an advocate of the abolition of slavery, or, say, foot binding, struck them ...

• BJCs are hard to design and continually update.

This objection is fair and reasonable, to my thinking. Any proposal has to be implementable, to be worth pursuing in any detail. If it is simply unworkable, then regardless of virtues, it has to be dumped. Still, BJCs would have to be awfully hard to design and maintain and upgrade for them to be a bad idea, given the tremendous virtues they have.

Nonetheless, with even a little tiny bit of thought, it seems to me obvious that this complaint too has no basis. OK, it is easier to design homogenous job complexes, I suppose. But marginally so. Because once you categorize tasks as being comparable to one another, and have a bunch of such categories, (and this is a prerequisite for having homogenous complexes), now creating a balanced job complex is merely a matter of taking tasks from various categories instead of taking them from only one, while (and this is presumably supposed to be the overwhelmingly hard part) being sure they can be handled in a smooth and sensible fashion, which is necessary in both events, and that the mix you choose is average.

And as far as maintaining the arrangement once it exists: in either case the advent of new tasks or new social arrangements means there is a need to redefine things.

But the critical point is that with hierarchical job complexes you need a vast store of repressive mechanisms to keep those below in line, which requires great attention and struggle, perverting relationships and misutilizing resources and energies. Whereas with BJCs, maintaining the system requires none of this. In short, if one cannot see that BJCs (once they exist and have been in place for a time) are far less difficult to maintain, one is, I think, blind to the existence of class difference and class struggle.

- How would your job change if your work institution were to balance job complexes internally?

How do you think it would change if complexes were then also balanced across all workplaces, with the economy as it is, other than this change?

- What would be the effect of introducing balanced job complexes into your workplace, now? What about as part of a national program that included retraining, etc.?

Well, my workplace does have BJCs. But it's probably safe to assume that such a change would have an enormous effect on your workplace.

- What would be the implication of having balanced job complexes in your workplace for the implementation of new technologies and other innovations?

Again, we have BJCs. As a result, our criteria for changing techniques, organization, or getting new software, are a comparison of the positive impact of the change on the nature of the work we have to do, or the speed with which we can do it, or on the quality of it, with the cost of implementing the change and any costs regarding the nature of work, speed of it, or quality of it.

The problem is, since most innovations depend on the outside world, like Microsoft and banks, there are limits on what our different values can accomplish.

- What is the relationship between having balanced job complexes in a good economy, and the process of deciding on investments and new technologies?

Because everyone is at a BJC, if there is an innovation in some workplace or industry, its impact is not confined to that site. Rather, if the quality of tasks at that site change for the better, there is a tiny overall improvement in average job complex throughout society. Everyone who works benefits to that degree. As a result everyone has the same interest when assessing possible technological or organizational innovations. Implement those innovations that have the largest and most desirable effects on output per effort and sacrifice, and on the quality of the societal average job complex.

It is interesting to try to figure out what this actually means in practice, and what a flexible and sane implementation of the idea would mean in terms of how changes occur and how balancing happens. You might want to pursue that line of reasoning.

> • Does having balanced job complexes oppress anyone, or
> reduce the well-being of anyone, as compared to having
> more traditional job arrangements?

As with any question like this (replace the phrase "having balanced job complexes" with "eliminating sexism" or "eliminating racism" or whatever else) there are two angles to view it from. What we think. And what the person who is in the position of losing the advantage is most likely to think.

Regarding the former, I think that the life situation of the person who is now free from onerous work may improve somewhat, on balance, from the switch that will cause them to have to do their share, on the one hand, but on the other free them from a degree of guilt and other ills associated with class division. But I wouldn't want to exaggerate this. A person who is now, let us say, a professor at an élite school, who earns $100,000 a year, who has a congenial work environment and who has huge resources at their disposal and who has minimal work responsibilities that are pretty much what the person would most like to be doing with their time in any event, really does have something to lose—in having to do a fair share of onerous and non-empowering work, and in having to have a fair income. And, yes, there are gains as well, very real and important ones.

As to what this person is likely to feel and how they are likely to react, I think that until there is a massive movement from below, and until the prospects of that movement winning are evident, those with advantages will give very little attention to the benefits that they will garner from change, but will focus instead on the disruption of their lives and the losses they will suffer.

And it raises an important strategic issue, which you might wish to begin to think about. Suppose, for the sake of the point, we think in terms of only working class, coordinator class, and capitalist class. Is the best way to improve life significantly in the foreseeable future to seek a goal that will alienate only capitalists, or one that will also alienate many in the coordinator class, or even aspiring to it?

• If you like the idea of job complexes, how would you reply to someone saying that they are unfair to very brilliant people, or impose too much responsibility on many people who won't want it?

Answered above.

• Do you have any idea at all what the organizational structure is and internal values are of political projects and institutions that you relate to or support? Why do you think you don't, assuming that is the case?

If you find the idea of balanced job complexes righteous and valid, or at least plausibly so, I wonder if you could hazard a guess as to why they are not a widely discussed programmatic aim among leftists?

I know the structure of those I am involved with, or that I have investigated. I believe the structure of most left organizations is not common knowledge, not something they make known publicly, and discuss and debate, for the obvious reason that it is nothing to brag about, and is, instead, in most instances little different from the structures that many of their verbal flourishes attack as despicable.

I believe BJCs are not a widely discussed aim among leftists because what is widely discussed on the left is that which appears in left publications, on left shows, in left teach-ins, or is promulgated by highly visible left figures. These, we can deduce, are not pushing this notion. I think it is easy to figure out why given the backgrounds and social circumstances of the people involved.

7. Consumption Institutions

Remuneration and consumption

"Annual income twenty pounds, annual expenditure nineteen pounds and six, result happiness. Annual income twenty pounds, annual expenditures twenty pounds ought and six, result misery."

—Charles Dickens

"I confess that I am not charmed with the ideal of life held out by those who think that the normal state of human beings is that of struggling to get on; that the trampling, crushing, elbowing, and treading on each other's heels, which form the existing type of social life, are the most desirable lot of human beings."

—John Stuart Mill

In this chapter we move on to our second discussion of consumption.

Consumption Institutions

I AM HELL-BENT ON GETTING YOU TO PARTICIPATE in thinking conceptually. At this point, if you have been keeping up with answering questions, you should be pretty well prepared to do so, I think. And if not, there is no time like the present to begin getting the most out of the process by trying to answer the questions on your own. So, regarding consumption:

- What is an externality of a consumption choice you may make, or action you may undertake? (In other words, an aspect that affects people beyond the buyer and seller.)

- What does the existence of consumption externalities imply about the process of arriving at consumption decisions given the desire for efficiency and given the desire for self-management?

- Are there different levels of consumption decision-making units, as with separate workers, work teams, plants and industries? If so, what implications does this have for how consumption should be undertaken?

- What should determine the volume of stuff I can consume in a year?

- What do I have to think about to decide what I want to consume?

- Can I just determine my preferences, or must they be agreed to by others? If so, who?

- Can I consume stuff that is going to hurt others? If not, what stops me from doing so? Suppose I am a drunk, for example?

- What protects personal rights and privacy of the consumer? What allows collective impact?

- How do you react to the following norms: (1) To guarantee equity there must be a measure of average per capita consumption for individuals, neighborhoods, regions, and states, and there must be a way to ensure that individuals, neighborhoods, regions, and states don't consume above the average amounts unless they receive permission from others to do so. Requests for goods and services that place an above average burden on society's productive potentials may be rejected by consumer councils on equity grounds. (2) To guarantee the right to privacy and personal control of one's purchases, average- and below-average requests must not be subject to oversight, and should they want to suffer the losses involved in forsaking the benefits of collective consumption goods, individuals must be free to act as their own one person consumption councils.

- Should it be possible to borrow and save? What would it mean in practice?

- Should one be able to increase one's consumption bundle above the social average? If so, how?

- What should be the relation between collective consumption requests and individual ones?

- What about someone who can't work? Do they consume? At what level?

- What reasons might influence your choice of a local area to live, that is, of a local consumption collective to become part of?

- Describe what you think might be an orderly and sensible routine that a person in a good economy might go through to plan their consumption for a year, then to update it periodically in light of changed preferences, circumstances, or expectations.

- Finally, please comment on the following passage from Ursula Leguin's *The Dispossessed*:

"Saemtenevia Prospect was two miles long, and it was a solid mass of things to buy, things for sale. Coats, dresses, gowns, robes, trousers, breeches, shirts, umbrellas, clothes to wear while sleeping, while swimming, while playing games, while at an afternoon party, while at an evening theatre, while riding horses, gardening, receiving guests, boating, dining, hunting—all different, all in hundreds of different cuts, styles, colors, textures, materials. Perfumes, clocks, lamps, statues, cosmetics, candles, pictures, cameras, hassocks, jewels, carpets, toothpicks, calendars, a baby's teeth rattle of platinum with a handle of rock crystal, an electrical machine to sharpen pencils, a wristwatch with diamond numerals, figurines and souvenir and kickshaws and mementos and gewgaws and bric-a-brac, everything either useless to begin with or ornamented so as to disguise its use; acres of luxuries, acres of excrement. After one block, Shevek had felt utterly exhausted. He could not look any more. He wanted to hide his eyes. But to Shevek the strangest thing about the nightmare street was that none of the millions of things for sale were made there. They were only sold there. Where were the workmen, the miners, the weavers, the chemists, the carvers, the dyers, the designers, the machinists, where were the hands, the people who made? Out of sight, somewhere else. Behind walls. All the people in all the shops were either buyers or sellers. They had no relation to the things but that of possessions. How was he to know what a goods' production entailed? How could they expect him to decide if he wanted something? The whole experience was totally bewildering. Were his hosts in this strange world, the 'shoppers' of A-lo, really capable of such daily acts of social irresponsibility?"

ANSWERS TO QUESTIONS

"Viewed as a body of substantive hypotheses, theory is to be judged by its predictive power for the class of phenomena which it is intended to 'explain.'"

—Milton Friedman

- What is an externality of a consumption choice you may make, or action you may undertake?

Any effect of the choice or action whose consequences are felt by other than solely the buyer and/or seller. I get vodka, consume it, and this affects my housemates. If I get seeds and plant a garden, my neighbor gets a beautiful eye full. I get toys, consume them, and dispense with them as I get older—they are plastic and degrade the environment.

- What does the existence of consumption externalities imply about the process of arriving at consumption decisions given the desire for efficiency and given the desire for self-management?

The people affected by outcomes are supposed to be proportionately involved in making them. If there is an externality to some economic choice, then the decision must be made with input from people other than just the buyer and seller.

If this is not done, then of course there will be no participatory self-management. But, likewise, if it is not done decisions may be made which have harmful effects on non-buyers and sellers that are much greater than any positive effects buyers or sellers may enjoy. In other words, from the broader perspective of all people's well-being and development, many choices that buyers and sellers make in light only of effects on themselves may be less than optimal, or even horrible.

- Are there different levels of consumption decision-making units, as with separate workers, work teams, plants and industries? If so, what implications does this have for how consumption should be undertaken?

It seems to me that there is the individual, the smallest living unit, the next larger size living unit (perhaps extended family or commune, or whatever), then the neighborhood, county, and so on.

There are certain consumption choices that are primarily relevant to a single actor, or some larger collective. The decision process needs to reflect this, both in terms of the impact we have on choices, and in terms of charging people properly for their fair share of costs.

So, if my family or my commune gets a lot of collective goods, each member is going to be charged a fair share and have less for individual goods.

- What should determine the volume of stuff I can consume in a year?

I would say the overall social product, and then how much above or below the average outlay of effort and sacrifice I have contributed to its creation—unless I have some good reason why I couldn't contribute, in which case I get the average by right, or some compelling reason why I should get more than average, in which case, if granted, I get that.

- What do I have to think about to decide what I want to consume?

Certainly my own preferences. But also the effects of my choices on other people, both immediately around me, and also at a distance, such as the people who will have to produce what I seek to consume. Partly this is straight solidarity and empathy. Partly it is also self-interest. It is pointless for me to say I want some commodity that involves onerous work, if I really don't care for it all that much. Why? It reduces overall work quality for everyone, myself included, to behave in such a way.

- Can I just determine my preferences, or must they be agreed to by others? If so, who?

Of course I determine my preferences. Who the hell else would?

- Can I consume stuff that is going to hurt others, if not, what stops me from doing so? Suppose I am a drunk, for example.

This is a very tricky matter. Everybody's will is manifest in the prices of items, via the social planning process. Likewise, workers have a proportionate say in what they will do. But a lot of this happens at the level of gross supply and demand, and people's individual reactions to it. What might be a perfectly sensible order for Vodka, for the country, for a region, even for a local neighborhood or commune, could conceal a horrible order for some individual.

What happens? Now we have two competing values at stake. Privacy and proportionate self-management. I have a right to privacy regarding my desires, etc. But my community has a right to step in when my personal consumption choices are threatening the community or some or all of its members. Suppose I like manufacturing bombs as a hobby, or, at a lesser level, drinking myself into a violent state.

What Hahnel and I came up with when we were thinking about parecon and asking just these types of questions was that individuals could submit their consumption proposals anonymously. This way the proposals are seen, and can be challenged, yet the person's privacy isn't abridged. More, except in the most extreme cases, though an individual's private choices of how to spend their budget can be challenged, if can't be abridged. For the latter degree of intervention, there would have to be special cause.

So the answer is kind of mixed. If what I want is produced, and available, and I have sufficient budget to afford it (at its real price), I can have it. But, my neighbors can also challenge consumption proposals that seem anti-social. And, in special cases, even intercede.

- What protects personal rights and the privacy of the consumer? What allows collective impact?

Well, with our answer above, this is pretty clear: anonymity and freedom to spend up to your budget level as you choose, on the one hand, and the right to intercession, on the other.

- How do you react to the following norms: To guarantee equity there must be a measure of average per capita consumption for individuals, neighborhoods, regions, and states, and there must be a way to ensure that individuals, neighborhoods, regions, and states don't consume above the average amounts unless they receive permission from others to do so. Requests for goods and services that place an above average burden on society's productive potentials may be rejected by consumer councils on equity grounds.

These seem fair to me, obviously. But let me throw in a thought-provoking wrinkle. Supposing we want equal outcomes, not in some crass material sense, but in the sense of equal personal fulfillment and development for all. Should everyone have the same budget? If I am bigger, I need more food. If I get my fulfillment and pleasure from playing violin, and you from playing harmonica, why do I have to pay more of my total income for the same outcome (fulfillment and pleasure) that you pay less for. What do people think about this fly in the ointment? Is it, or isn't it?

> • How do you react to the following norms: To guarantee the right to privacy and personal control of one's purchases, average- and below-average requests must not be subject to oversight, and should they want to suffer the losses involved in forsaking the benefits of collective consumption goods, individuals must be free to act as their own one person consumption councils.

Makes sense to me. As a last resort, you vote with your feet. If you don't like parecon, don't take its offerings, don't abide its limitations, either in part, or in full.

> • Should it be possible to borrow and save? What would it mean in practice?

I can't see any problem with allowing this. To think there needs to be equity every minute is a fetish, to my mind, and grossly inflexible, whether we are talking about roles or income. So why shouldn't I be able to spend some of next year's income earlier, or to save some for the future?

But this does introduce tricky problems. For any durable good I would ever buy, of course I would like to buy it now rather than later, to get the pleasure of its use for a longer time during my life. Well, everybody cannot do this. We can't all be working later for our hamburger today, to quote the meat-eating bozo in *Popeye*. So something to think about is the exact norms and mechanisms of saving and borrowing.

> • Should one be able to increase one's consumption bundle above the social average? If so, how?

If I exert more effort and give more of myself (sacrifice), sure, I ought to be able to receive more of the social product back in return. It is hard to see how anyone could do this to too great a degree, however.

Suppose the average work week is 30 hours. Could someone manage to get 30 extra hours of labor at balanced job complexes consistently with everybody else's plans? Would anyone want this? I don't know, but I doubt it would cause any real problems for the system. If it would, however, then there would have to be norms about how much "overtime" people could work.

• What should be the relation between collective consumption requests and individual ones?

Seems like the collective consumption requests that I benefit from, I in part pay for. Also, it makes little sense for me to arrive at individual requests before I know what my collective units are getting. It could easily change my situation and personal preferences. So it is entwined, in the budget sense, and I think the collective request is prior, in the planning sense.

• What about someone who can't work? Do they consume? At what level?

Well, what else, they starve? It seems to me that they get an average budget, that they can consume as they wish. In fact, the way I like to think of parecon is that everyone gets an average budget by right of being a person.

Everyone also has a responsibility to work an average job complex an average length of time. The two things are separate at the level of right and responsibility, but linked at the level of "amount." Anyone who wants to can, on top of this normal situation, petition for some more income, less work, or whatever. What determines whether the petition is granted? Partly its value and logic. Partly whether the person helps pay for its implementation by additional effort and sacrifice. This way labor and income are only operationally linked for the part that diverges from average.

• What reasons might influence your choice of a local area to live, that is, of a local consumption collective to become part of?

The personalities of people, of course, but also their collective goods preferences. Depending on my preferences I might like a group that spends a lot on musical instruments and practice rooms, or on an observatory and lab, or on one that has various kinds of athletic equipment, and so on. In other words, it make sense to choose where one lives on a variety of grounds including proximity to work, family and friends, climate, etc., but also the collective goods preferences of people in various size living groups.

> • Describe what you think might be an orderly and sensible routine that a person in a good economy might go through to plan their consumption for a year, then to update it periodically in light of changed preferences, circumstances, or expectations?

I'm going to leave this one for later chapters.

> • Comment on the passage from Ursula Leguin's *The Dispossessed* ...

What can I say? She understands things that ninety-five percent of professional economists are one hundred percent oblivious to. But then, so does the average person on the street. Leguin does, however, say it better.

8. Allocation Institutions

Considering information and organization

"Once upon a time there was a magnet, and in its close neighborhood lived some steel filings. One day two or three filings felt a sudden desire to go and visit the magnet, and they began to talk of what a pleasant thing it would be to do. Other filings nearby overheard their conversation, and they, too, became infected with the same desire. Still others joined them, till at last all the filings began to discuss the matter, and more and more their vague desire grew into an impulse. 'Why not go today?' said some of them; but others were of the opinion that it would be better to wait until tomorrow. Meanwhile, without their having noticed it, they had been involuntarily moving nearer to the magnet, which lay there quite still, apparently taking no heed of them. And so they went on discussing, all the time insensibly drawing nearer to their neighbor; and the more they talked, the more they felt the impulse growing stronger, till the more impatient ones declared that they would go that day, whatever the rest did. Some were heard to say that it was their duty to visit the magnet, and that they ought to have gone long ago. And, while they talked, they moved always nearer and nearer, without realizing they had moved. Then, at last, the impatient ones prevailed, and, with one irresistible impulse, the whole body cried out, 'There is no use waiting. We will go today. We will go now.

We will go at once.' And then in one unanimous mass they swept along, and in another moment were clinging fast to the magnet on every side. Then the magnet smiled—for the steel filings had no doubt at all but that they were paying that visit on their own free will."

—Oscar Wilde

In this chapter we begin an extended discussion of allocation institutions.

INFORMATION AND ALLOCATION

THIS TIME I DECIDED TO USE A MORE TEXTUAL chapter, and to make it a slightly adapted version of chapter 4 from the book Hahnel and I wrote published by Princeton University Press. The chapter title is "Allocation," and it is a statement of what participatory allocation is, written for professional economists. (There are a couple of related mathematical chapters too, but this chapter appears here essentially as it appeared there.) I think you will have few problems with this chapter, and it will help to indicate the difference between a conversational chapter, and an effort to present similar content in a more precise fashion. These types of "professional" presentation actually have little to do with the process of conceptualizing vision, or analyses, for that matter. They are after the fact. In the rest of the chapters, I try to be more true to the kinds of thinking and procedures typical of conception, as compared to presentation. But this provides a good contrast, I think, and also does manage to present the allocation system in a succinct way.

Here we describe an alternative system of allocation, called decentralized participatory planning. The system permits consumers and workers councils to participate directly in formulating a plan and has strong egalitarian properties. Because workers and consumers councils propose and revise their own activities prior to initiating those activities, the planning process is a decentralized, social, iterative procedure.

We consider specifying this procedure and analyzing its welfare theoretic properties our most important contribution to developing a libertarian economic vision (along with the idea of balanced job complexes, and its implications, I think I would add). The idea of "associated producers" democratically determining their own plan is no more original to us than the vision of workers and consumers councils. But whereas many before us have contributed to the theory of the internal workings of democratic councils, few have attempted to explain, in detail, how those councils might jointly settle on a plan. In fact, most economists agree no third procedure qualitatively different from markets and central planning exists, or, if there is another alternative, that it has not been articulated at a level permitting meaningful comparison with markets and central planning.

Alec Nove, for example, threw down the gauntlet in unequivocal terms: "I feel increasingly ill-disposed towards those who ... substitute for hard thinking an image of a world in which there would be no economic problems at all (or where any problems that might arise would be handled smoothly by the 'associated producers' ... In a complex industrial economy the interrelation between its parts can be based in principle either on freely chosen negotiated contracts [i.e. markets], or on a system of binding instructions from planning offices [i.e. central planning]. There is no third way." Allen Buchanan posed the challenge in a somewhat more agnostic vein: "It is impossible to show that a feasible non-market system at least approaches the productivity of the market unless (1) a rather well-developed theoretical model of the non-market system is available, and (2) it is demonstrated that a sufficiently productive approximation of the ideal system described in the theoretical model is practically possible. Unfortunately, [no one] has achieved even the first step—that of providing a theoretical model for a non-market system."

In this chapter we present a rebuttal to Nove and a direct answer to Buchanan by providing a "rather well-developed" theoretical model of a decentralized planning procedure and offering a preliminary analysis of its efficiency properties as well as arguing that "a sufficiently productive approximation of the ideal ... system described in the theoretical model is practically possible," including description of a number of experiments through which other economists might sensibly test this claim.

PARTICIPATORY INFORMATION AND COMMUNICATION

Our description of participatory workers and consumers councils (in prior chapters) assumed that the necessary information about their relations with others would be available. But what precisely do workers in a council need to know to regulate their production activity cognizant of the effects on themselves, other workers, and consumers? And what must consumers know to formulate their consumption requests in light of their own needs as well as the needs of other consumers and workers?

Participatory workers must be able to weigh the gains from working less or employing less productive though more fulfilling techniques against the consequent loss of consumer well-being. Participatory consumers need to be able to weigh the gains of a consumption request against the sacrifices required to produce it. Participatory workers must be able to distinguish an equitable work load from one that is too light or too heavy. And participatory consumers need to be able to distinguish reasonable consumption demands from ones that are unreasonable or overly modest. Finally, all actors must know the true social costs and benefits of things they demand or supply, that is, all the non-human and human, quantifiable and non-quantifiable consequences of their choices, if they are going to participate in informed collective self-management.

FIRST COMMUNICATIVE TOOL: PRICES

Prices providing accurate estimates of the full social costs and benefits of inputs and outputs are the most important quantitative communicative tools we use. They arise in the process of participatory planning and serve as guides to proposals and evaluations. And this is an important point.

All too often theoretical economists view "efficiency" prices or "shadow" prices as quantitative measures that can be found via technical procedures. In the literature on central planning, for example, shadow prices arise as the solution to what is called the dual of the primal planning problem that central planners "solve." And in neoclassical literature on market systems, an equilibrium price vector is studied as something implied by preferences and technologies taken as givens. While these conceptions are useful in some regards, they are misleading as well. Real people's preferences arise in social communicative processes. Not only do results depend on what those processes are like, but the very preferences that lie at the basis of the results depend on the processes as well. So, without engaging in undue mystification, we should remember that estimates of social costs and benefits with any claim to accuracy must arise from social, communicative processes. The trick is to organize these processes so people have no incentives to dissimulate regarding their true desires, and all have equal opportunity to manifest their feelings. It is precisely because our participatory planning process is different from the flawed communicative processes of market and centrally planned allocation that the prices to which it gives rise will be different as well.

In any case, prices are "indicative" during the planning process in the sense of indicating the best current estimates of final valuations. They are not binding but flexible in the sense that qualitative information provides important additional guidance. And they are not the product of competition or authoritarian determinations, but of social consultation and compromise. The idea is that qualitative information is necessary if quantitative indicators are to be kept as accurate as possible. But qualitative information is also necessary to develop workers' sensitivity to fellow workers' situations and everyone's understanding of the intricate tapestry of human relations that determines what we can and cannot consume or produce. So both to ensure accuracy and to foster solidarity we need a continual, social resetting of prices in light of updated qualitative information about work lives and consumption activity. Thus, the cybernetic burden of a participatory allocation procedure is considerably greater than for non-participatory economies.

Not only must a participatory economy generate and revise accurate quantitative measures of social costs and benefits in light of changing conditions, but it must communicate substantial qualitative information about others' conditions as well.

SECOND COMMUNICATIVE TOOL: MEASURES OF WORK

As we explained earlier, job complexes are balanced in each workplace, and in plants with above-average work conditions workers spend time doing more menial tasks elsewhere, while in plants with below-average work conditions, people put time into more interesting pursuits elsewhere.

For an individual to work more or less than the social average in a given period and not disrupt a humane balance of work, she or he need only diminish or increase her or his hours worked at all tasks in the same proportion. Then, each individual could receive from her or his workplace an indicator of average labor hours expended as an accurate indicator of work contributed.

Over a sufficient period, whenever a person's indicator was high (or low) compared to the social average, the individual would have sacrificed more (or less) for the social good, and would be entitled to ask for proportionately more (or less) consumption in return. This is unlike what emerges from the Marxist labor theory of value:

In our system job complexes are balanced by a real social evaluation, and our "hour counts" serve only as guidelines for decisions since councils can grant exceptions for higher (or lower) consumption requests as conditions and needs warrant.

In short, participatory planning can obtain a reasonable first estimate of effort expended by counting labor hours because people's job complexes have been balanced. These estimates can then be revised in light of effort intensity ratings by one's work mates. In attempting to gain consumption flexibility, only unbalancing job complexes is prohibited.

THIRD COMMUNICATIVE TOOL: QUALITATIVE ACTIVITY

To guard against "reductionist accounting" each actor needs access to a list of everything that goes into producing goods directly and indirectly, and a description of what will be gained from consuming them. This means those who produce and consume particular goods must try to communicate the qualitative human effects that cannot be captured in quantitative indicators. This does not entail everyone writing novel-length reports about their work and living conditions. It does mean generating concise accounts that substitute for the fact that not everyone can personally experience every circumstance.

Of course, not every worker and consumer will use all this qualitative information in all calculations. But over time people will become familiar with the "congealed" material, human, and social components of products they use just as people are now familiar with the products themselves. In this way, everyone can more accurately assess the full effects of others' requests in a way that enhances solidarity. Both producers and consumers must therefore receive not only quantitative summaries of overall social costs and benefits, but detailed qualitative accounts as well. Only this will ensure that the human and social dimensions of economic decision-making are not lost, and guarantee that summary price data remains as accurate as possible.

ALLOCATION ORGANIZATION

"When we should have been planning switches to smaller, more fuel efficient, lighter cars in the late 1960s, in response to a growing demand in the marketplace, GM refused because 'we make more money on big cars.' It mattered not that customers wanted the smaller cars, or that a national balance of payments deficit was being built.... Refusal to enter the small car market when the profits were better on bigger cars, despite the needs of the public and the national economy, was not an isolated case of corporate insensitivity. It was typical."

—John DeLorean, former head of Pontiac Division at GM

Every workplace and neighborhood consumers' council participates in the social, iterative procedure we call participatory planning. But besides workplace councils, we also have industry councils and regional federations of workers' councils. And besides neighborhood consumers' councils, we also have ward, city, county, and state federations of consumers' councils as well as a national consumers' council. Moreover, in addition to all these councils and federations of councils, various facilitation boards assess collective proposals and large-scale investment projects, regional and industry boards assist workers changing places of employment, and household boards help individuals and families find membership in living units and neighborhoods. Finally, at every level of the economy facilitation boards help units revise proposals and search out the least disruptive ways of modifying plans in response to unforeseen circumstances.

In our companion volume, *Looking Forward* (South End Press, 1991), we provide comprehensive descriptions of planning institutions and procedures, including hypothetical case studies for particular kinds of workplaces and consumers' councils intended to illustrate the texture of participatory planning.

Here we present a summary of results sufficient for theoretical purposes.

PARTICIPATORY PLANNING

- Each consumption "actor" proposes a consumption plan.
- Individuals make proposals for private goods.
- Neighborhood councils make proposals that include approved requests for private goods as well as the neighborhood's collective consumption request. Higher level federations make proposals that include approved requests from member councils as well as the federation's collective consumption request.
- Similarly, each production "actor" proposes a production plan. Workplaces enumerate the inputs they want and outputs they will make available. Regional and industry federations aggregate proposals and keep track of excess supply and demand.
- Every actor at every level proposes its own plan, and, after receiving information regarding other actors' proposals and the response of other actors to its proposal, each actor makes a new proposal.
- As every actor "bargains" through successive "iterations," the process converges.

PREPARING FIRST PROPOSALS

The real world always has a "just completed year." If production and consumption of the just completed year was recorded, we would have information about last year's plan for each actor. If the prices used to calculate social costs, benefits, and income last year were recorded, we have a set of "indicative prices" that could be used to begin this year's estimates as well. By storing last year's full plan in a central computer, access to relevant parts including indicative prices could be made available to all actors in the planning process. Additionally, each unit knows what its own proposals were in each iteration last year.

So, how do workers' and consumers' councils plan?

1. They use relevant data from the previous year.

2. They receive information from facilitation boards estimating the coming year's probable changes in prices and income in light of existing knowledge of past investment decisions and changes in the labor force.

3. They receive information from higher level production and consumption councils regarding long-term investment projects or collective consumption proposals already agreed to in previous plans that imply commitments for this year.

4. By reviewing changes in their own proposals made during last year's planning they assess how much they had to scale down their consumption desires or their plans to improve the quality of work life, and look to see what increases in average income and improvements in the quality of average work complexes are projected this year over last.

5. Using last year's final prices as indicators of social costs and benefits they develop a proposal for the coming year, not only enumerating what they want to consume or produce—and implicitly what they think society's total output should be—but also providing qualitative information about their reasons.

This does not mean units must specify how many units of every single good they need down to size, style, and color. Goods and services are grouped into classes accordingly as they are roughly interchangeable regarding the resources, intermediate goods, and labor required to make them. For planning purposes we need only request types, even though later everyone will pick an exact size, style, and color. Individuals present consumption requests to neighborhood councils where they are approved or disapproved. Once approved, individual consumption requests are summed and added to the neighborhood collective consumption request to become the neighborhood consumption proposal. These in turn are summed with consumption requests from other neighborhoods into ward proposals, which are summed along with consumption requests from other wards into city proposals. Having the next higher level council review, approve, or contest lower level requests until they are ready to be passed on saves a great deal of planning time.

In the same way, a firm's iteration board provides all its workers with summaries of last year's production schedule, including what was initially proposed, changes made during planning iterations, and what was (finally) approved, as well as a prediction of this year's requests based on extrapolations from new demographic data and the trajectory of last year's iterations. Individual workers consider this information, discuss ideas for improving the quality of work life, and enter proposals which are averaged into the firm's first proposal for "inputs" and "outputs." After some number of iterations, firm proposals are discussed, negotiated, and decided as a unit rather than each individual making his or her own proposal and these being averaged.

Besides quantitative proposals for each production and consumption unit, a qualitative addenda including descriptions of changes in circumstances and conditions is also entered into the computerized planning system. At any point any council can access the data banks of any facilitation board and any other council.

Proceeding From One Proposal to Another

The first proposals are in. We have all answered how much we want to work and consume in light of our own presumably over-optimistic assessments of possibilities. Do the proposals constitute a plan, or must we have another round? To decide, it is only necessary to sum all proposals and compare total demand and total supply for every class of final good and service, intermediate good, and primary input. In a first iteration, where consumers propose in part a "wish list" and workers propose substantial improvements in their work lives, while some goods may be in excess supply, for most goods initial proposals should generate excess demand. In other words, initial proposals are not supposed to sum to a feasible plan.

As the next step, every council receives new information indicating which goods are in excess supply or demand by what percentage, and how its proposal compares to those of other relevant units. Most important, iteration boards provide new estimates of indicative prices projected to equilibrate supply and demand.

At this point, consumers reassess their requests in light of the new prices and most often "shift" their requests for goods in excess demand toward goods whose relative prices have fallen because they were in excess supply or less in excess demand than others. Consumers' councils whose overall requests were higher than average would also be under pressure to "whittle down" their requests in hopes of winning approval. Equity and efficiency emerge simultaneously. The need to win approval from other similar councils forces councils whose per capita consumption request is significantly above the social average to reduce their overall requests. But the need to reduce can be alleviated by substituting goods whose indicative prices have fallen for those whose prices have risen. Attention focuses on the degree to which units diverge from current and projected averages, and on whether their reasons for doing so are compelling.

Similarly workers' councils whose ratios of social benefits of outputs to social costs of inputs were lower than average would come under pressure to increase either efficiency or effort, or to explain why the quantitative indicators are misleading in their particular case. Before increasing their work commitment, workers would try to substitute inputs whose indicative prices had fallen for inputs whose indicative prices had risen, and substitute outputs whose indicative prices had risen for outputs whose indicative prices had fallen.

Each iteration yields a new set of proposed activities for all economic actors. Once summed, these yield new data regarding the status of each good and the average consumption per person and production "benefit cost ratio" per firm. All this allows calculation of new price projections and new predictions for average income and work, which in turn lead to modifications in proposals until excess demands are eliminated and a feasible plan is reached.

FLEXIBLE UPDATING

Converging and updating are related because both can benefit from algorithms that take advantage of the large scale of the planning process. Assume we have settled on a plan for the year. Why might we need to update it during the year, and how might this be done with least disruption.

Consumers begin the year with a working plan including how much of different kinds of food, clothing, meals at restaurants, trips, books, records, and tickets to performances they will consume. What if someone wants to substitute one item for a slightly different one? Or what if she wants to delete or add entries? Or what if she changes her mind and wants to save or borrow more than planned? She belongs to a neighborhood consumers' council which in turn belongs to a ward council, a city federation, and so on. Some changes will cancel out among all the consumers within the neighborhood, others will cancel out at the ward level, and so on. As long as adjustments by many consumers cancel at some consumption federation level, production plans need not change. Indeed, making adjustments without disrupting production plans is one function of consumer federation boards.

But what happens if aggregate demand rises for some good? Suppose individuals record their consumption on "credit card" computers that automatically compare the percentage of annual requests "drawn down" with the fraction of the year that has passed, taking account of predictable irregularities such as birth dates and holidays.

This data can be processed by planning terminals which communicate projected changes to relevant industry councils which in turn communicate changes to particular firms. The "technology" involved is little different from the now common system of computerized store inventories where cash register sales are automatically subtracted from inventory stocks. In any case, what would then happen is that consumer federations, industry councils, and individual work units would engage in a dialogue to negotiate adjustments. Such dialogues may lead to work diminishing in some industries and increasing in others, including possible transfers of employees, but there need be no more moving about than in other types of economies. In any case, the need for workers to change jobs or increase or diminish work loads would be a factor considered in the dialogue over whether to meet changed demands.

However, since each firm's activities have implications for other firms, if planned matches between supply and demand are calculated too closely, any change in demand could disrupt the whole economy. For this reason a "taut" plan would prove unnecessarily inconvenient since it would require excessive debating and moving. To avoid this and to simplify updating, the plan agreed to should include some excess supply for most goods. A practical knowledge of those industries most likely to be affected by non-averaging alterations would facilitate this type of "slack planning."

CONVERGING TO A PLAN

A little thought reveals that convergence can be a complicated matter. Adjusting indicative prices to reduce excess supplies and demands is more complicated in practice than in economists' theoretical models with all their convenient assumptions. For example, a product in excess demand in one iteration could overshoot equilibrium and be in excess supply in the next iteration as workers offer to produce more and consumers offer to request less in response to a price increase. Worse still, considering that each product's status affects the status of many others, progress in one industry could disrupt equilibrium in another. Theoreticians' solutions to these headaches always assume away the troublesome phenomena. Whether the issue is market equilibrium and stability or convergence of iterative planning procedures, it is well known that convexity and gross substitutability assumptions are good aspirin for these theoretical headaches. But simplifying assumptions are no aspirin at all for practitioners operating in the real world.

To make our participatory planning procedure more efficient, specific economies will incorporate flexible rules that facilitate convergence in a reasonable time but do not unduly bias outcomes or subvert equity. Procedures can range from rote algorithms carried out by computer that take short cuts toward equilibrium, to rules that prohibit actors' responses that would yield time consuming loops, to adjustments fashioned and implemented by specialized workers experienced in facilitating convergence when particular situations arise. Devising and choosing from among these and other possibilities is a practical issue in implementing any actual participatory economy. Assuming the procedures chosen do not violate principles essential to participatory planning, considerations include:

1. The extent to which iteration workers could bias outcomes;
2. The extent of reductions in the number of iterations required to reach a plan;
3. The amount of planning time saved through compartmentalizing subsets of iterations; and
4. How much less onerous to producers and consumers their calculations could be made.

A Typical Planning Process

Since the procedure we have described is dramatically different from traditional market and central planning allocation, it is useful to summarize by describing what a typical planning process might look and feel like to its participants.

The first step is for each individual to think about her or his plan for the year. Individuals know they will end up working in a balanced job complex, and can expect to consume an average consumption bundle unless their work effort is above or below normal or special needs dictate otherwise. The first decision is whether they want to "save" by working longer or consuming less than average, or "borrow" by working less or consuming more than average. Facilitation boards provide an initial estimate of what average consumption and average work loads will be for the year based on last year's levels, last year's investments in equipment and training, and adjustments that occurred during last year's iterations. When you make your first proposal you are not only proposing to do specific work and consume specific items, but you are proposing a level of work contribution and consumption request for yourself, and, implicitly, at least on average, for everyone else as well. To be realistic you must coordinate your work and consumption proposals, though you need not agree with facilitation board growth estimates.

In other words, what you propose is: "I would like to work so much at my job complex and to consume so much broken down in the following way." And this proposal is based on last year's experience, your prediction of economic growth, and your individual decision about saving and borrowing. Everyone makes such a choice, trying to optimize given their particular preferences and within the constraint that the overall amount consumed must be produced and that responsibilities and rewards in this endeavor will be distributed equitably.

After first proposals are summed, new indicative prices are calculated and new projections of social averages estimated. Note that it would not even be possible to implement most initial production proposals since in most firms one person in a team may have proposed working more hours than another person in the same team, even though they can only work together. Moreover, most goods will be in excess demand so the initial plan is infeasible as well.

Again every individual would formulate a new response. You compare your proposed work load and proposed consumption to the average proposals of others. You might also consider more localized averages, for example in your firm or industry, and in your council or neighborhood. You certainly consider the status of each item you ordered or proposed since excess demands and supplies will be reflected in changes in indicative prices. That is, you will be faced with summaries of the statuses of goods as well as new estimates of social opportunity costs and benefits. After you consult descriptive explanations for what seems odd to you, like large changes in worker productivity or consumer choice, and after you consult with whomever you like and whatever data you are interested in, you then make any desired changes before entering your second proposals. And, once again, all these new proposals are summed and the new information made available for the third iteration.

So far there have been no rules or limits on workers' or consumers' responses. Now, however, there could be a change. Instead of being able to change proposals in any direction by any amount, limits might be imposed. For example, consumers might be prohibited from increasing their demand for certain goods beyond some maximum percentage above projected averages for the economy. Or producers might be prevented from lowering output proposals by more than some percent in this and subsequent rounds.

The point is simply that it is possible to impose rules limiting changes to specific ranges to keep the status of goods from varying excessively from round to round. Any particular implementation of participatory planning settles on socially desirable and mechanically efficient rules to guide the behavior of producers and consumers in different iterations.

In the third or fourth iteration, proposals might be limited to councils instead of individuals. Consumers meet in their local neighborhood councils and workers in their workplace councils to settle on council-wide proposals so that work proposals are no longer abstract unimplimentable averages but consistent work plans that could be enacted if inputs requested were made available.

Note that nothing about our procedures pushes different actors to consume the same amounts of different goods.

Individual consumers and producers can hold pat on proposals that are far from average. On the other hand, workplaces do feel pressure to measure up to average "benefit cost ratios," and consumers will be pressured to keep their overall requests from exceeding average income. Indeed, at this stage production councils that persist, after allowance for acknowledged different circumstances, in proposals with benefit cost ratios below their industry's average, might have to petition their industry for permission not to be disbanded. And, similarly, although again with sensible allowances, local consumers' councils with above average proposals might have to petition higher federations explaining special circumstances to warrant their requests.

The fifth iteration in our hypothetical procedure might deploy still another rule to accelerate planning. This time facilitation boards extrapolate from the previous iterations to provide five different final plans that could be reached by the iterative process. What distinguishes the five plans is that each entails slightly different total product, work expended, average consumption, and average investment. All actors then vote, as units, for one of these five feasible plans. Each plan is a consistent whole and implimentable. Once one of the five is chosen as the base operating plan, units adjust requests in subsequent iterations in conformity with the base plan until individual agreements are also reached.

CONCLUSION

While we must still address important aspects of participatory allocation, it is useful to summarize here where our argument stands. We have argued earlier that hierarchical production and consumption, markets, and central planning are individually and in combination incompatible with efficient, egalitarian, economies in which people control their own lives and enjoy solidarity. We have also presented a description of participatory, nonhierarchical production and a description of participatory, equitable consumption. In this chapter we have described a planning procedure that promotes participation, equity, solidarity, and diversity and supports rather than undermines participatory production and consumption within units.

QUESTIONS ABOUT ALLOCATION

"I never would believe that Providence had sent a few rich men into the world, ready booted and spurred to ride, and millions ready saddled and bridled to be ridden."

—Richard Rumbold

Here are some questions taking off from the material presented above. "Participatory workers must be able to weigh the gains from working less or employing less productive though more fulfilling techniques, against the consequent loss of consumer well-being. Participatory consumers need to be able to weigh the gains of a consumption request against the sacrifices required to produce it. Participatory workers must be able to distinguish an equitable work load from one that is too light or too heavy. And participatory consumers need to be able to distinguish reasonable consumption demands from ones that are unreasonable or overly modest. Finally, all actors must know the true social costs and benefits of things they demand or supply, that is, all the non-human and human, quantifiable and non-quantifiable consequences of their choices, if they are going to participate in informed collective self-management."

- Is this acceptable? Does this seem like an accurate accounting of what is needed to have a good allocation communications system? Do you have different ideas for an economy you would like?

- What are prices for, in any economy? What do we do with them? When are prices useful and worthwhile? What attributes make some prices harmful? Why do we call our prices "indicative prices" instead of simply prices?

"So, without engaging in undue mystification, we should remember that estimates of social costs and benefits with any claim to accuracy must arise from social, communicative processes. The trick is to organize these processes so people have no incentives to dissimulate regarding their true desires, and all have equal opportunity to manifest their feelings. It is precisely because our participatory planning process is different from the flawed communicative processes of market and centrally planned allocation that the prices to which it gives rise will be different as well."

- What the hell does the above paragraph mean?

"The idea is that qualitative information is necessary if quantitative indicators are to be kept as accurate as possible. But qualitative information is also necessary to develop workers' sensitivity to fellow workers' situations and everyone's understanding of the intricate tapestry of human relations that determines what we can and cannot consume or produce. So both to ensure accuracy and to foster solidarity we need a continual, social resetting of prices in light of updated qualitative information about work lives and consumption activity. Thus, the cybernetic burden of a participatory allocation procedure is considerably greater than for non-participatory economies. Not only must a participatory economy generate and revise accurate quantitative measures of social costs and benefits in light of changing conditions, but it must communicate substantial qualitative information about others' conditions as well."

- What is different about this view, and the one typical of our own society? Is the above view OK with you?

"In short, participatory planning can obtain a reasonable first estimate of effort expended by counting labor hours because people's job complexes have been balanced. These estimates can then be revised in light of effort intensity ratings by one's work mates. In attempting to gain consumption flexibility, only unbalancing job complexes is prohibited."

- What does that mean, in practice? And is it acceptable to you?

"To guard against 'reductionist accounting' each actor needs access to a list of everything that goes into producing goods directly and indirectly, and a description of what will be gained from consuming them."

- Why? And under what conditions do we need this? How often? What does this information look like and how is it to be communicated? What is going on here, methodologically, in trying to figure out a vision?

- What is a council? Of what use are they? What kind do I propose we have in a good economy? Do you agree or not, and why? How diverse can they be in their structure? What constraints operate on them? Are councils part and parcel of real participation and democracy, or an obstacle to it?

- What is a facilitation board? What do they do? Why? Are these functions necessary? Is there a better way to get them done? What requirements do we need to place on institutions that facilitate planning? Who would work in them?

With what perks and problems?

"Each consumption actor proposes a consumption plan."

- Fine. Who are the "actors" and what constitutes such a proposed plan? Is there a better way to go?

"Similarly, each production actor proposes a production plan."

- Again, who are the actors, and what constitutes such a proposed plan? Does it make sense?

- How do the consumers' first proposals likely compare with the producers' first proposals? Why? What would we think if what was proposed as output was greater than what people said they wanted for input? What is to be done about discrepancies? Does participatory planning seem like a sensible approach? Would it be better to circumvent the hassle using a central planning approach, or a market approach?

- What does it mean to say that to start planning for this year, workers and consumers councils "access relevant data from the previous year"? Why? How does this help? What pitfalls are involved with taking this approach?

- Why do they next "receive information from facilitation boards estimating this year's probable changes in prices and income in light of existing knowledge of past investment decisions and changes in the labor force?" Are there problems with this?

- And why do "they receive information from higher level production and consumption councils regarding long-term investment projects or collective consumption proposals already agreed to in previous plans that imply commitments for this year?" Also, does this mean there is some center making decisions for everybody else?

- What are they learning when "by reviewing changes in their own proposals made during last year's planning they assess how much they had to scale down their consumption desires or their plans to improve the quality of work life, and look to see what increases in average income and improvements in the quality of average work complexes are projected this year over last"?

- How do the actors develop proposals for the coming year? What do they take into account? What calculations and judgments do they engage in?

• What degree of detail does a proposal embody?

"In the same way, a firm's iteration board provides all its workers with summaries of last year's production schedule, including what was initially proposed, changes made during planning iterations, and what was (finally) approved, as well as a prediction of this year's requests based on extrapolations from new demographic data and the trajectory of last year's iterations. Individual workers consider this information, discuss ideas for improving the quality of work life, and enter proposals which are averaged into the firm's first proposal for "inputs" and "outputs." After some number of iterations, firm proposals are discussed, negotiated, and decided as a unit rather than each individual making his or her own proposal and these being averaged. Besides quantitative proposals for each production and consumption unit, a qualitative addenda including descriptions of changes in circumstances and conditions is also entered into the computerized planning system. At any point any council can access the data banks of any facilitation board and any other council."

> • Either defend or critique this from the point of view of values you believe in. Does it embody the values I have been touting?
> • With the first proposals in, how do we know whether they constitute a plan or not?
> • What is the next step for each actor—consumers, producers, and facilitation boards?

"The need to win approval from other similar councils forces councils whose per capita consumption request is significantly above the social average to reduce their overall requests. But the need to reduce can be alleviated by substituting goods whose indicative prices have fallen for those whose prices have risen. Attention focuses on the degree to which units diverge from current and projected averages, and on whether their reasons for doing so are compelling."

> • Is this good? Why or why not?

"Similarly, workers' councils whose ratios of social benefits of outputs to social costs of inputs were lower than average would come under pressure to increase either efficiency or effort, or to explain why the quantitative indicators are misleading in their particular case. Before increasing their work commitment, workers would try to substitute inputs whose indicative prices had fallen for inputs whose indicative prices had risen, and substitute outputs whose indicative prices had risen for outputs whose indicative prices had fallen."

- What does this mean? Does it seem positive or negative to you?

- What is a planning iteration, and explain why parecon does or doesn't converge to a plan, and to desirable outcomes? Suppose in practice it seems to converge too slowly. What would be your reaction?

- To what extent is society bound by the plan it initially establishes? To what extent can final outcomes diverge from those planned? How does this happen?

- What is the role of slack planning? What kinds of things do we know in advance that enable us to be prepared for deviations between what people say they want, and what, in fact, they likely will want?

"A little thought reveals that convergence can be a complicated matter. Adjusting indicative prices to reduce excess supplies and demands is more complicated in practice than in economists' theoretical models with all their convenient assumptions. For example, a product in excess demand in one iteration could overshoot equilibrium and be in excess supply in the next iteration as workers offer to produce more and consumers offer to request less in response to a price increase. Worse still, considering that each product's status affects the status of many others, progress in one industry could disrupt equilibrium in another. Theoreticians' solutions to these headaches always assume away the troublesome phenomena. Whether the issue is market equilibrium and stability or convergence of iterative planning procedures, it is well known that convexity and gross substitutability assumptions are good aspirin for these theoretical headaches. But simplifying assumptions are no aspirin at all for practitioners operating in the real world."

- So what is to be done about this?

- Please summarize in your own words what a typical planning process might look and feel like to its participants. And please comment on whether you think this is a good use of the individual's energies or not, a good way to allocate or not? And, if you think not, please note if you have any ideas for improvements, or for an alternative approach.

- What is the relation between balanced job complexes and

participatory planning and remuneration according to effort and sacrifice? Are these independent options, or do they relate to one another in some deeper way?

· What do you like about parecon? What worries you about it?

Answers to (Some of) Our Questions

"Reason, or the ratio of all we have already known, is not the same that it shall be when we know more."

—William Blake

Hahnel and I wrote: "Participatory workers must be able to weigh the gains from working less or employing less productive though more fulfilling techniques, against the consequent loss of consumer well-being. Participatory consumers need to be able to weigh the gains of a consumption request against the sacrifices required to produce it. Participatory workers must be able to distinguish an equitable work load from one that is too light or too heavy. And participatory consumers need to be able to distinguish reasonable consumption demands from ones that are unreasonable or overly modest. Finally, all actors must know the true social costs and benefits of things they demand or supply, that is, all the nonhuman and human, quantifiable and non-quantifiable consequences of their choices, if they are going to participate in informed collective self-management."

· Is this acceptable? Does this seem like an accurate accounting of what is needed to have a good allocation communications system? Do you have different ideas for an economy you would like?

Yes, it seems to me like an accurate accounting. I have few ideas beyond what is in the books. In fact, when I think about it I realize that since writing them, while I have spent much time answering questions or reacting to confusions and criticisms, I have had almost no time to spend thinking about enriching the vision, or refining it, or augmenting it. Strange. But then why shouldn't others do that, in any event?

· What are prices for, in any economy? What do we do with them? When are prices useful and worthwhile? What at-

tributes make some prices harmful? Why do we call our
prices "indicative prices" instead of simply prices?

Prices are to provide information to help actors make choices as part
of the allocation process. We register them, and then make our choices
in light of implications, in part clarified by knowing prices.

Prices are useful and worthwhile when they help us make decisions that truly reflect our desires and capacities and accurately
account for those of others, and for broader implications. Prices are
better or worse, therefore, to the degree that they convey an accurate
(if very summary) representation of the relative costs and benefits of
options. They are harmful when they systematically and inexorably
misrepresent costs and benefits, particularly if always in the same direction, as with the way market prices misrepresent externalities and
social goods.

We call our prices "indicative" to emphasize that they are information we use alongside other information, and that they are products of a social process designed to provide useful information and not
a power struggle designed to have winners and losers.

Hahnel and I wrote: "So, without engaging in undue mystification, we should remember that estimates of social costs and benefits
with any claim to accuracy must arise from social, communicative
processes. The trick is to organize these processes so people have no
incentives to dissimulate regarding their true desires, and all have equal
opportunity to manifest their feelings. It is precisely because our participatory planning process is different from the flawed communicative processes of market and centrally planned allocation that the prices
to which it gives rise will be different as well."

• What the hell does the above paragraph mean?

If prices emerge from a process that is supposed to allow each actor to
express their preferences and desires and have these accounted for proportionately as the actor is affected, then it is key that the process
gives actors no reason to misrepresent themselves and provides them
every means to know their own true interests and feelings. We claim
parecon has these qualities. If it doesn't, then it needs to be corrected,
or replaced.

Hahnel and I also wrote: "The idea is that qualitative information
is necessary if quantitative indicators are to be kept as accurate as possible. But qualitative information is also necessary to develop workers'
sensitivity to fellow workers' situations and everyone's understanding

of the intricate tapestry of human relations that determines what we can and cannot consume or produce. So both to assure accuracy and to foster solidarity we need a continual, social resetting of prices in light of updated qualitative information about work lives and consumption activity. Thus, the cybernetic burden of a participatory allocation procedure is considerably greater than for non-participatory economies. Not only must a participatory economy generate and revise accurate quantitative measures of social costs and benefits in light of changing conditions, but it must communicate substantial qualitative information about others' conditions as well."

 • What is different about this view, and the one typical of our own society? Is the above view OK with you?

In our society the qualitative information that is passed in the allocation process (in market exchanges) has as its purpose getting someone to do something regardless of the merit of their doing so. Thus we have ads aimed at getting someone to buy something, regardless of their need for it. The goal isn't helping someone to do what they wish, in light of true knowledge. It is getting someone to buy, regardless of whether it will help the person, please them, or whatever. Thus ads are generally manipulative, full of lies, and so on. Notice: In parecon producers never want people to purchase what they produce other than if they are really going to benefit from it. There is no incentive to want to increase sales for their own sake. (Think about most book publishers now. What do they care about? Number of books sold, or impact of the books? Well, what does the best seller list measure …)

And Hahnel and I wrote: "In short, participatory planning can obtain a reasonable first estimate of effort expended by counting labor hours because people's job complexes have been balanced. These estimates can then be revised in light of effort intensity ratings by one's work mates. In attempting to gain consumption flexibility, only unbalancing job complexes is prohibited."

 • What does that mean, in practice? And is it acceptable to you?

I think what it means in practice is what I describe in theory, with a degree of practical flexibility. And yes, it is quite OK with me.

And Hahnel and I wrote: "To guard against 'reductionist accounting' each actor needs access to a list of everything that goes into producing goods directly and indirectly, and a description of what will be gained from consuming them."

- Why? And under what conditions do we need this? How often? What does this information look like and how is it to be communicated? What is going on here, methodologically, in trying to figure out a vision?

In fact, I think the sentence is overstated. We need to be able to do this, and to do it often enough so we are in touch with the reality of production and consumption and how it works and its broad effects, and the real meaning of the numbers we call indicative prices, and so on. But we don't need to do it for every item, and all the time.

It is really part of a general learning process, developing knowledge of the economy as well as a procedure for checking things out when one's inclinations and prices or requests seem out of whack and one wants to know why, in more detail.

I think the information is qualitative, descriptive, and is communicated in words by telecommunications, of course. What is going on, methodologically, is we are trying to figure out what kinds of structural processes, steps, and information must be utilized for allocation to have the properties we want for it.

- What is a council? Of what use are they? What kind do I propose we have in a good economy? Do you agree or not, and why? How diverse can they be in their structure? What constraints operate on them? Are councils part and parcel of real participation and democracy, or an obstacle to it?

A council is a set of relations among a bunch of people. They allow bunches of people to make collective decisions that are not simply the sum of each person's individual decisions. Thus, for example, decisions about workplace organization, say, or collective goods consumption. I propose that we have councils that are effective means for arriving at group decisions in ways compatible with our overarching values—solidarity, equity, self-management, diversity. There are many different ways to attain this, I suspect, and choosing among them may be largely a matter of the size and role of the council, of the preferences of its members, of the types of decisions under review. Councils are an essential ingredient of real democracy, it seems to me.

- What is a facilitation board? What do they do? Why? Are these functions necessary? Is there a better way to get them done? What requirements do we need to place on institutions that facilitate planning? Who would work in them? With what perks and problems?

A facilitation board is a workplace whose product is information and data useful for people trying to participate in the participatory planning process. Therefore, facilitation boards amass data and present it in accessible format. I think the critical requirement of these institutions is that they function within the norms of the economy, consistent with its values. One could imagine additional requirements, but I doubt any additional ones are necessary because I do not see any compelling way for people working in these institutions to aggrandize themselves at the expense of others. Only people who wanted to work in them would do so. The perks and problems, as with any other workplace, would be those associated with the tasks involved in the work. The workers would have balanced job complexes, of course.

Hahnel and I wrote, "each consumption actor proposes a consumption plan." I also said "Similarly, each production 'actor' proposes a production plan."

> • Fine. Who are the "actors" and what constitutes such a proposed plan? Is there a better way to go?

Consumers and consumer units and councils, and likewise producers and producers' units, councils.

> • How do the consumers' first proposals likely compare with the producers' first proposals? Why? What would we think if what was proposed as output was greater than what people said they wanted for input? What is to be done about discrepancies? Does participatory planning seem like a sensible approach? Would it be better to circumvent the hassle via a central planning approach, or a market approach?

Consumers first proposals should seek more than producers first proposals offer to produce because both are supposed to ask for their ideal preferred options. I would think that people were curbing their requests unduly, and exaggerating their desires to work unduly, if we had opposite outcomes.

Discrepancies are reduced by way of the allocation planning process. That is its purpose. The problem with the central planning approach is that even if we assume a benign planner, with omniscient insight into what is needed, we still don't have people making decisions in proportion as they are affected by them. In practice, of course, a central planner with disproportionate powers will be neither benign nor all-knowing. The problem with the market solution, however competitive, is that it arrives at answers by a process that is biased in various ways (for example, against public goods) thus yielding bad outcomes, as well as denying proportionate say.

The additional problem is that in practice both these modes of allocation produce class division.

> • What does it mean to say that to start planning for this year, workers and consumers councils "use relevant data from the previous year"? Why? How does this help? What pitfalls are involved with taking this approach?

It means we have knowledge of last year's plan to use as a starting point in thinking about what we wish to do this year. We can modify in light of changes in technology, population, or our own tastes. The problem is we could have a mistake from one year affect the next year.

> • Why do they next "receive information from facilitation boards estimating this year's probable changes in prices and income in light of existing knowledge of past investment decisions and changes in the labor force"? Are there problems with this?

We know our budget from last year. We get information that lets us figure out what it would be with the same level of work this year. Then we can make intelligent decisions about whether we want to work the same level, more, or less.

> • And why do "they receive information from higher level production and consumption councils regarding long-term investment projects or collective consumption proposals already agreed to in previous plans that imply commitments for this year?" Also, does this mean there is some center making decisions for everybody else?

Part of my income is spent on collective goods. I need to know this both because it reduces the amount left to spend on individual items, and because the content of the collective goods consumption affects what I need. If I have a ball field coming to my neighborhood, or a gym or library, it has implications.

> • What are they learning when "by reviewing changes in their own proposals made during last year's planning they assess how much they had to scale down their consumption desires or their plans to improve the quality of work life, and look to see what increases in average income and improvements in the quality of average work complexes are projected this year over last?"

People are learning what is possible, what is desired, and how they match up, for others, and for themselves.

> • How do the actors develop proposals for the coming year? What do they take into account? What calculations and judgments do they engage in?

I figure my desires and tastes against my preference for leisure time and against knowledge of changing prices and budgets. I create a new proposal for this year by altering last year's, I would think. I am calculating what my budget is, how much I want to work, how much I want different possible items, and so on.

> • What degree of detail does a proposal embody?

This is a subtle question. Statistics are powerful things. Suppose we know the demand for shirts. Can we then calculate how many of each size and style, based on past knowledge? Suppose we know the demand for nuts, grossly. Can we then calculate details? And so on. Much of the detail of daily consumption does not need to be arrived at in the global plan. The more so as an economy is intentionally structured to reduce the need for details.

> • With the first proposals in, how do we know whether they constitute a plan or not?

Does amount desired match amount proposed to be produced, for every good, within an acceptable fudge factor level?

Hahnel and I wrote: "The need to win approval from other similar councils forces councils whose per capita consumption request is significantly above the social average to reduce their overall requests. But the need to reduce can be alleviated by substituting goods whose indicative prices have fallen for those whose prices have risen. Attention focuses on the degree to which units diverge from current and projected averages, and on whether their reasons for doing so are compelling."

> • Is this good? Why or why not?

Yes, I think it is precisely what's needed. It is a kind of dynamic process, a pressure, that causes all the actors in the system to move their proposals toward a stable plan. And yet, each is continually guided by ever more accurate information, and his or her own preferences.

And Hahnel and I wrote: "Similarly workers' councils whose ratios of social benefits of outputs to social costs of inputs were lower than average would come under pressure to increase either efficiency or effort, or to explain why the quantitative indicators are misleading in their particular case. Before increasing their work commitment, workers would try to substitute inputs whose indicative prices had fallen for inputs whose indicative prices had risen, and substitute outputs whose indicative prices had risen for outputs whose indicative prices had fallen."

• What does this mean? Does it seem positive or negative to you?

It is just an elaborate way to talk about trying to get some job done at the least cost. Yes, it seems positive to me, given that the quantitative indicators employed account for all social affects.

• What is a planning iteration, and explain why parecon does or doesn't converge to a plan and to desirable outcomes? Suppose in practice it seems to converge too slowly. What would be your reaction?

An iteration is just a round of negotiating in the planning process. The system converges because at each step all actors have information and incentives to move toward convergence. If it is too slow, we would need to find ways to speed the process, without subverting its virtues. But for me "too slow" is relative and I would think a reasonable amount of time given to planning economic life would be quite acceptable, especially given the reduction in time previously needed for many tasks that would be eliminated from life under the new economy.

9. Evaluating Economic Vision

How do we evaluate vision?

"It is necessary, with bold spirit and in good conscience, to save civilization.... We must halt the dissolution that corrupts the roots of human society. The bare and barren tree can be made green again. Are we not ready?"

—Antonio Gramsci

"An hour's listening disclosed the fanatical intolerance of minds sealed against new ideas, new facts, new feelings, new attitudes, new hints at ways to live. They denounced books they had never read, people they had never known, ideas they could never understand, and doctrines whose names they could not pronounce. Communism, instead of making them leap forward with fire in their hearts to become masters of ideas and life, had frozen them at an even lower level of ignorance than had been theirs before they met Communism."

—Richard Wright

EVALUATING PARECON

I THINK THIS IS REALLY NOT FOR ME TO DO. I would like to have the reader do this, based on methods and lessons learned, and your own inclinations. Let me simply provide some minimal guidance.

Evaluating any economy means describing one's criteria of value, and then determining to what extent the economy fulfills these. For example, suppose one is most concerned about ecological sanity, or equity between races, or—well—whatever. Then one assesses the economy asking how its dynamics fulfill or deny the values in question.

Also, one might compare the economy to others, on the same axes of valuation.

If you want to evaluate parecon, for example, I think it entails deciding what you value, what you want an economy to accomplish, and then assessing whether parecon measures up, in general, and compared to other economic models, by examining its core institutions for production, consumption, and allocation and determining their implications for the values you favor.

ECONOMIC VISION IN SOCIETY

"Let me say, with the risk of appearing ridiculous, that the true revolutionary is guided by strong feelings of love.... Above all, always be capable of feeling any injustice committed against anyone anywhere in the world."

—Che Guevara

What have we done so far in this book to develop an economic vision? We've thought about some basic defining features—production, consumption, allocation. We've established goals for each but also knew that whatever choice we made for any one feature had to be compatible with choices for other features.

Thus, the needs of production and what it provides have to fit the needs of consumption and what it provides, and both have to fit the needs of allocation and what it provides. And this has to be true not just for the flow of material goods, say, or even labor, but also for types of consciousness, skills, values, and so on. You can't have workplace democracy and councils and balanced job complexes in each production unit if the production units exist in context of a market or central planning allocation system that creates class division. You can't have participatory planning with equitable remuneration if you have workplaces that are organized hierarchically, thereby creating class interests. To return to an earlier analogy, this is like trying to put together a stereo from components and picking speakers and an amplifier that are mismatched in that the speakers require more power than the amplifier can deliver, or the amplifier delivers too much power for the speakers to handle.

The same holds for the defining features of a society. We can decide on aims for an economy, but we must also recognize that our economy has to intertwine with a kinship sphere (where the issues of procreation and socializing the next generation are handled), cultural sphere (where the issues of community identification and celebration are handled), and political sphere (where the issues of political decision making and adjudication are handled). And each of these has to be at least compatible with the rest. It can't be that one critical side of life requires attributes squelched by others, or that one produces attributes contrary to others. Knowing one sphere, we can't deduce the rest. But we can come to some conclusions about attributes other spheres must have to be compatible. So, knowing that we want a parecon, we can deduce some qualities that other spheres will have to have to be compatible with the economy. And the same holds the other way, too, if we develop a vision for other spheres of social life.

So here are my questions, as a way to guide and provoke conceptualizing broader vision.

- What are some goals you would like to see attained by a revolutionized kinship sphere. What implications would this have for an economy, and is parecon compatible?
- What are some goals you would like to see attained by a revolutionized cultural sphere. What implications would this have for an economy, and is parecon compatible?
- What are some goals you would like to see attained by a revolutionized political sphere. What implications would this have for an economy, and is parecon compatible?
- Finally, what implications do you think having a parecon has for accompanying kinship, cultural, or political spheres?

ANSWERS TO QUESTIONS

"Disciples do own onto masters only a temporary belief and a suspension of their own judgement until they be fully instructed, and not an absolute resignation or perpetual captivity."

—Francis Bacon

• What are some goals you would like to see attained by a revolutionized kinship sphere. What implications would this have for an economy, and is parecon compatible?

First, how would one approach this question in a disciplined fashion? Well I don't think it is different in method from what we have tried to do in the prior chapters. One needs to decide basic aims for kinship. Then one needs to figure out basic concepts, first what is the kinship sphere, then what are its component institutional functions. Next, we might evaluate existing models and proposals for kinship structures using our values. Ultimately, we have to try to conceive new institutions (or choose among existing ones we like) and construct a model for the sphere out of favored options.

When I think about this, it seems to me that kinship institutions should impose no distinctions on men and women, or adults and children, or people of different sexual preference that are biologically unnecessary or contrary to full development and fulfillment of all these actors. There should be no opposed interests for the groups, or any other groups. When I think about kinship roles, I conclude that attaining these aims requires, ultimately, an end to the nuclear family, an end, in fact, to the whole idea of gender-defined asymmetrical mothering and fathering—as compared to gender-neutral parenting. That said, one can conceive many ways that people might court, procreate, and socialize, all consistent with desirable social values and outcomes.

I think the implications, in both directions, are in general relatively easy to describe. Each sphere of social life has to have no implications for actors that are contrary to basic operations in any other sphere. So, the economy cannot demarcate among men and women, or any other constituencies, in ways that would make kinship institutions inoperable. This would certainly happen if the economy enriched men and impoverished women, for example. In the same way, however, the kinship sphere, and thus socialization institutions, etc., have to provide people with habits, beliefs, skills, knowledge, and personalities suited to participation in a parecon.

- What are some goals you would like to see attained by a revolutionized cultural sphere. What implications would this have for an economy, and is parecon compatible?

Following the usual procedure, I find myself favoring something I call "intercommunalism." The idea is simple enough. There is no right culture. The notion that everyone should have a correct culture is a cultural nightmare (though typically it is the view of many marxists). Instead, there ought to be many cultures, which is to say, many cultural communities. These may be defined in many ways, including religion, geography, various types of taste and preference and belief. Intercommunalism is a situation in which every cultural community is free to pursue its beliefs and customs and celebrations as it likes, and is provided by right the space and means to do so, and is protected by right in any dispute with any larger cultural community. The large community gives way, that is, to the small: an intellectually trivial but profoundly important practical requirement, I think.

The economy will, to be compatible, have to treat all people identically, whatever their cultural allegiances. More, it will have to welcome cultural community caucuses to ensure that the culture of economic institutions and practices are not oppressive to minority groups. There is nothing in parecon that I can see that would disrupt intercommunalism, and much that would augment and foster it.

10. Reactions to Parecon

How do parecon's authors respond to criticisms offered of the parecon vision?

"Works are of value only if they give rise to better ones."
—Von Humboldt

In this final chapter I would like to present some of the debate that has taken place around the participatory economic model. To do this I include a (slightly amended) essay Robin Hahnel and I wrote in answer to some economist critics. It summarizes a variety of weaknesses attributed to parecon, and answers them as best we are able to.

WHY PARTICIPATORY PLANNING?

IN THE SHADOW OF SOVIET TURMOIL, AND VERY FAR from the public eye, a debate over what is a *desirable* economy has rekindled among those who believe people deserve more than capitalism. In the past five years a small torrent of books and articles have appeared. *Science and Society* and the *Review of Radical Political Economics* have both published special issues on the debate, *Z Magazine* has published a symposium, Pen-L (a progressive economists' Internet Forum) has facilitated spontaneous interchanges by modem, and periodic conferences of academics and activists have hosted the debate on panels in numerous cities. Participants have divided into two schools—proponents of "market socialism" versus proponents of democratic or "participatory planning"—with important differences of opinion within both camps. As an active partisan in these discussions, we would like to:

1. Restate our criticisms of market models that have not been adequately addressed by marketeers

2. Defend participatory planning from frequent objections we do not find compelling, and

3. Note some serious issues proponents of participatory economies must ponder in light of questions that have been raised.

UNADDRESSED MARKET LIABILITIES

MARKETS ARE UNFAIR

The distributive maxim implicit in public enterprise market economies is "to each according to the social value of his or her labor." However, to the extent that productivity is the result of talent (the genetic lottery), education and training (frequently at public expense), or the quantity and quality of other productive inputs or of luck—rather than greater personal effort or sacrifice—payment according to productivity rewards people for things beyond their control and effort.

The inequity of some hard working people receiving lower wages and salaries than others who make lesser personal sacrifices but are lucky, have more education, are physically stronger, or work in better equipped factories, is unavoidable in any market economy. In a free market labor is paid at best and only roughly according to its marginal revenue product, which is the value the individual contributes to the product. But this usually differs significantly from the effort an individual expends. Moreover, within a market system any attempt to rectify the difference between what effort justifies and people's marginal productivities, *necessarily* leads to gross inefficiencies. Labor costs inevitably form a substantial portion of total production costs of most goods and services. In a market system, if wages are legislated to differ from productivities to make wages more equitable, labor costs, and consequently the entire cost structure of the economy, will deviate from true social opportunity costs. Since prices play an allocative role in every market model, this implies that any attempt to make wages more equitable must lead to significant allocative inefficiencies, even in a "market socialist" economy.

Some advocates of "market socialism" recognize and admit this liability. "A more just system of economic remuneration would arguably link payment solely to differential personal effort and personal sacrifice, not to the luck of the genetic draw." (Weisskopf 1992, page 8) And: "Even though our proposed system [market socialism] is likely to be more egalitarian than capitalism, there will be several departures from egalitarian distribution to the extent there are various incentive payment schemes for managers and workers." (Bardhan & Roemer, 1992, page 14) A few advocates of "market socialism" admit that the inequity in their system is not necessary for motivational efficiency any more than the inequity in capitalism is: "In market capitalist economies people are rewarded for productive contributions due to the property they own (in the form of capital income); such rewards to property ownership not only have very unequal distribution consequences, but they are generally not necessary to assure deployment of the property in production. In 'market socialist' economies people are rewarded primarily for productive contributions due to their own labor. Yet 'market socialism,' like capitalism maintains rewards to people's natural abilities (in the form of labor income), even though such rewards may not really be necessary to elicit the deployment of those abilities in production." (Weisskopf 1992, page 8)

Advocates who admit that "market socialism" is inequitable console themselves with the observation that capitalism is more inequitable, and the fact that progressive income taxes can ameliorate inequities: "While 'market socialist' systems do not achieve this ideal [payment according to effort], they do not depart from it anywhere near as much as do capitalist systems. Moreover, to the extent that unwarranted returns to a person due to their luck in the genetic lottery or in economic circumstances remain, the resulting differentials can be diminished by a progressive system of income taxation." (Weisskopf 1992, page 8)

Of course, the greater inequity of capitalism is not disputed by progressive critics of "market socialism." And it is important to also note that advocates of "market socialism" conveniently ignore the psychological and political obstacles to tax correctives, as well as the inefficiency that would accompany such intervention. Isn't it likely in a "market socialist" society that the economically advantaged would translate their advantages in wealth and leisure into disproportionate political power? And isn't it likely their disproportionate political power would be used to obstruct tax reforms to correct wage and salary inequities? Moreover, besides greater economic and political power to defend their advantages, opponents of corrective progressive taxation in "market socialist" societies would have two powerful arguments on their side. First, while progressive taxes on personal income do not initially disrupt allocative efficiency, they do create dynamic, or motivational inefficiency in a system that relies heavily on material incentives—as conservative opponents of progressive taxation have correctly pointed out in capitalist economies. Second, and more important in our view, people inevitably tend to rationalize their behavior. The logic of the labor market is: she or he who contributes more gets more. When people participate in the labor market they must defend their right to a wage on the basis of their contribution. The logic of redistribution through progressive taxation contradicts this operating logic. So participation in "market socialist" labor markets not only does not lead people to see the justice of progressive taxation, it inclines them to accept the argument of its opponents, which is: "Everyone already got what they contributed, so any after-the-fact redistribution would be unfair."

There is a further ethical dilemma in "market socialism." Advocates of social democracy and "market socialism" invariably treat education as a fundamental human right and champion universal public education as a cornerstone needed to guarantee equality of economic opportunity and a democratic polity. We agree. But what is the sense of permitting individuals to appropriate the benefits of greater productivity that comes from education and training—which they will in "market socialism"—if the cost of that education and training is born at public expense? Market logic requires either that individuals bear the expense of education from which they reap the benefits in the form of higher wages and salaries, or that education at public expense not give rise to private benefits. But efficiency precludes the latter possibility in "market socialism." It is therefore unclear how social democrats can wrap themselves in the mantel of generous universal public education and sing the praises of markets as well, without serious inconsistency.

CLASS DIVISIONS

We have claimed on numerous occasions that "markets create a social environment in which a class of managers, professionals, intellectuals and technicians—who we call coordinators—increasingly dominate and ultimately exploit ordinary workers." (Albert and Hahnel, 1992a, page 47) And some advocates of "market socialism" even admit this is the case. "It is certainly true that under 'market socialism' there must be some people occupying positions of key decision-making responsibility, and in all likelihood such people will have higher incomes as well as greater power than most of the rest of the population.... There would be ample scope for inequalities associated with differential skills, talents and responsibilities." (Weisskopf 1992, page 9)

To quote another advocate of "market socialism" speaking more broadly: "If democratic governance is a value, it seems reasonable to favor institutions that foster the development of people likely to support democratic institutions and able to function effectively in a democratic environment. Among the traits most students of the subject consider essential are the ability to process and communicate complex information, to make collective decisions, and the capacity to feel empathy and solidarity with others. As we have seen, markets may provide a hostile environment for the cultivation of these traits. Feelings of solidarity are more likely to flourish where economic relationships are ongoing and personal, rather than fleeting and anonymous; and where a concern for the needs of others is an integral part of the institutions governing economic life. The complex decision-making and information processing skills required of the modern democratic citizen are not likely to be fostered in either markets or in workplaces that run from the top down." (Bowles, 1991, page 16) Bowles' main point here is that markets are not the training grounds for political democracy they are advertised to be in the mainstream equation of political democracy with free market economics. But the dearth of "complex decision-making and information processing skills" as well as empathy generated in market economies, and particularly the unequal distribution of these traits among participants, are precisely what make market systems breeding grounds for what we call "coordinator class" dynamics and distinctions.

As with inequity, the defense mounted by advocates of "market socialism" is not to deny that "market socialism" fosters class differentiation, but to point out that the class inequalities would be less than those in capitalism, and to suggest that class differentiation is inevitable in any event. "Although a market system could not assure anything close to full equality of income and power for all participants, neither could any economic system in a complex society. Such societies require sophisticated decision-making institutions of one kind or another; and there are bound to be great differences among people in their ability (or desire) to participate effectively in decision-making processes." (Weisskopf 1992, page 9)

While we agree that differential economic power and class distinctions are inevitable in "market socialism," we believe specific features of a participatory economy make formation of classes unlikely, even impossible, as we discuss below. Ironically, those like Weisskopf who are pessimistic about the possibilities of ever eliminating unequal decision-making power are also among the first to criticize features of a participatory economy designed to minimize unequal economic power as infringing on individual freedoms. More, the claim that "it can't be done" is never substantiated with evidence or analysis. It is a kind of a priori impossibility theorem. Life is complex, therefore, says the pessimist, we must incorporate oppressive structures—though perhaps a bit less oppressive than in the past. One might just as easily say, a bit more optimistically, life is complex, therefore, among its vast possibilities we should seek and attain the liberating ones, rejecting those that are oppressive. The point is, the only way one knows what is possible and what isn't is to think carefully on the matter, and, ultimately, try the alternatives.

ANTISOCIAL

While Bowles concludes his recent discussion of the pros and cons of markets with a plea for regulation rather than a call for a superior allocative mechanism, and while the sentiments he expresses about markets' antisocial bias are very reminiscent of arguments we have made elsewhere (Albert and Hahnel, 1978; 1981, and Hahnel and Albert, Chapter 7, 1990), we quote him because it is more significant when these problems are admitted by a defender of markets than espoused by market bashers like ourselves.

Bowles writes: "Even if market allocations did yield pareto-optimal results, and even if the resulting income distribution was thought to be fair (two very big "ifs,") the market would still fail if it supported an undemocratic structure of power or if it rewarded greed, opportunism, political passivity, and indifference toward others. The central idea here is that our evaluation of markets—and with it the concept of market failure—must be expanded to include the effects of markets on both the structure of power and the process of human development." (Bowles, 1991, page 11) He continues: "The beauty of the market, some would say, is precisely this: It works well even if people are indifferent toward one another. And it does not require complex communication or even trust among its participants. But that is also the problem. The economy—its markets, workplaces and other sites—is a gigantic school. Its rewards encourage the development of particular skills and attitudes while other potentials lay fallow or atrophy. We learn to function in these environments, and in so doing become someone we might not have become in a different setting." (Bowles, 1991, page 13)

Bowles concludes: "By economizing on valuable traits—feelings of solidarity with others, the ability to empathize, the capacity for complex communication and collective decision making, for example—markets are said to cope with the scarcity of these worthy traits. But in the long run markets contribute to their erosion and even disappearance. What looks like a hardheaded adaptation to the infirmity of human nature may in fact be part of the problem." (Bowles, 1991, page 13)

Quite simply, we couldn't agree more. We have been playing these themes for close to two decades to largely empty houses. And we also agree with Weisskopf: "Don't market systems systematically undermine efforts to serve the general public interests? Markets provide an environment in which people are encouraged to find ways to better themselves at the expense of others." (Weisskopf 1992, page 8) And: "To transact effectively in markets, people do have to think mainly in terms of their own individual (or family) welfare, while setting aside consideration for others; markets encourage anonymity, autonomy and mobility rather than community, empathy and solidarity. 'Market socialism' thus admittedly does not provide direct support for a culture of community, empathy, and solidarity." (Weisskopf 1992, page 9)

But Weisskopf offers rebuttal to his own criticism: "This line of reasoning is theoretically plausible; yet it is not decisive. Rent seeking behavior and self-aggrandizing coalitions of one kind or another can and will occur under any conceivable system of economic organization that permits some people to live better than others. Virtually every system will therefore require institutions that limit antisocial behavior. The only way in which an economic system of organization per se could eradicate the problem would be if that system, by virtue of its controls on individual patterns of living, precluded any individual from enjoying the gains from self-interested behavior. Thus a solution to the problem of such behavior could come only at the price of strict limits on privacy and freedom of choice—a price that 'market socialists' are unwilling to pay." (Weisskopf 1992, page 8) (Of course, we deny this convenient "impossibility.") Weisskopf finishes with the usual observation that capitalism is much worse, anyway, and a prayer that non-economic institutions may save the day: "Yet ['market socialism'] surely does provide a less hostile environment for the development of empathy and solidarity than (market) capitalism…. [And] such [desirable personality] characteristics may be fostered in other spheres of life even in a market system." (Weisskopf 1992, page 10)

Let us state again, for the record, that "market socialism," or what we prefer to call "public enterprise market economies," are more desirable than market capitalism. We have no doubt that "to each according to personal contribution" is more equitable than "to each according to contribution of person and property." And employee-managed market economies obviously afford more opportunities for self-management than economies in which absentee owners manage the laboring capacities of others by means of hired henchmen. Moreover, the fact that advocates of "market socialism" are on the defensive in their debate with defenders of private ownership over the relative efficiency of the two systems is amusing. If employee-managed market regimes proved stable—that is, if the logic of competition and accumulation did not lead to a restoration of private ownership—we have no doubt they would prove more efficient as well as more equitable than capitalism. The motivational advantages of a greater degree of self-management in employee-managed systems is considerable. And the inefficiency and waste caused by the conflict between owners and employees in employer-managed systems is extensive as well. Moreover, claims that private capital markets are best suited to the task of weeding out those who are less adept at discovering and implementing innovations with the greatest net social benefits are preposterous on both logical and historical grounds. But this is not our major concern. We happily concede that employee-managed market economies (what our opponents call "market socialism") are more desirable than employer-managed market economies, that is, capitalism.

But in return for our unqualified support in their debate with pro-capitalists, we think it only honest for "market socialists" to concede that the superiority of "market socialism" over capitalism has no bearing on a debate over the relative desirability of "market socialism" and democratic or participatory planning. Comments to the effect that "market socialism" is more fair than capitalism, or more democratic than capitalism, or more efficient than capitalism, carry no weight in a debate over whether participatory economies or "market socialist" economies are more equitable, democratic, or efficient. And we also fail to see why it should be of any comfort that non-economic institutions may prove more supportive of solidarity and democracy than markets. Logically it is just as possible that markets undermine solidarity and community in other spheres of social life as it is that solidaritous dynamics elsewhere will ameliorate the antisocial effects of markets. And as far as evidence is concerned, our sense of the last five hundred years of history, aided by the insights of Karl Polanyi and countless anthropological studies, make the former hypothesis far more plausible.

But, is it true, as Weisskopf claims, that "rent seeking behavior and self-aggrandizing coalitions of one kind or another can and will occur under any conceivable system of economic organization" so this problem is not due to markets but is a fact of economic life?

Certainly Homo Economus (an entity motivated by purely pecuniary and personal calculation and which most economists assume all people are)—who is well represented by the law firm of Micro, Neoclassico, and Marketo—can be counted on to check out these possibilities in any system she or he is put in, including a participatory economy (to be discussed below). But in market economies there are two avenues to self-aggrandizement: One is through socially beneficial behavior such as discovering and producing goods and services that others like rather than dislike, or discovering and implementing techniques that lower social costs of production. Adam Smith studied the beneficial logic of voluntary exchange long ago and dubbed it the "invisible hand." But market economies offer another route to self-aggrandizement, namely advancing one's interests at the expense of the interests of others. Smith believed, erroneously, that competitive market structures and full information closed down this second route to self-aggrandizement, thereby securing the invisible hand. In actual practice, however, while competitive conditions diminish opportunities to pursue this route of self-advancement by providing others who one might disadvantage opportunities for exit, this does not eliminate a multitude of opportunities for self-advancement in market economies which are socially counter productive. E.K. Hunt pointed to externalities as a plentiful source for such opportunities, identified externalities as the Achilles heel of market economies with respect to efficiency, and dubbed the dynamic whereby markets provide incentives for socially counter-productive individual advancement the "invisible foot" (Hunt and D'Arge, 1973). Environmental economists such as Jacobs have used the term "invisible elbow." We have explained elsewhere why political economists should expect externalities to be much more prevalent than neoclassical economists admit, and why recognizing that people's preferences are endogenous magnifies the socially counter-productive potentials of Hunt's invisible foot and Jacobs' invisible elbow. (Hahnel and Albert, Chapters 6 and 7, 1990)

Still, Weisskopf is right that in a system that not only relies exclusively on material self-aggrandizement as the means of motivating behavior, but aggressively penalizes any and all failures to do so, socially counter-productive, "rent seeking" behavior will occur unless there are "institutions that limit antisocial behavior." But there are two insuperable obstacles to erecting adequate corrective institutions of this kind in market economies. First, there are too many holes in the market system dike. That is, as Hunt demonstrates, the solution of creating new markets in the external effects is no solution at all and actually compounds the problem. These effects are everywhere. And we have demonstrated that any conceivably adequate system of incentive compatible mechanisms for dealing with the ubiquitous public effects of private actions would transform a market system into something bearing little resemblance to a "free market" economy. (Hahnel and Albert, 1990, chapter 7) Second, any institution that closed down a socially counter-productive avenue of self-advancement would also undermine people's motivation to innovate, invest, or work in a market economy.

In short, the "human" logic of market economies is very simple: They dangle opportunities for individuals to capture rents before people's eyes. If people are permitted to capture those rents both inequities and inefficiencies result. But if people are prevented from capturing those rents (by well designed institutions that limit antisocial behavior) there is little reason for people to play the market game. How can "socialist" marketeers pretend to have their cake and eat it too?

But this is not an answer to Weisskopf's argument above. He does not deny this dilemma exists in market economies—although he does not go out of his way to highlight it either. Instead he asserts that this problem exists in "any conceivable system of economic organization that permits some people to live better than others," and implies that any system which did not permit some people to live better than others is undesirably restrictive of "privacy and freedom of choice." We will take up these issues below in the context of a participatory economy. But we can state here that participatory economies were designed in large part: to reduce to a minimum (if possible to zero) the possibility of socially counter productive self-advancement; to prevent some people from "living better" than others unless they had undergone greater personal sacrifice (in which case you might say they do not live better than others in the overall context); and to accomplish these ends without any infringement on privacy and freedom other than when necessary to prevent a greater infringement on the privacy or freedom of others.

INEFFICIENCY

In the *Review of Radical Political Economics* special issue on "The Future of Socialism" we stated the case regarding efficiency politely: "Received wisdom not withstanding, markets allocate resources very inefficiently." (Albert and Hahnel, 1992a, page 47) We will summarize the reasons here again so "market socialists" can explain which of our arguments and or assumptions they dispute.

1. Rather than exceptions, external effects (where parties external to a transaction are affected by the transaction) are the rule. The prevalence and unevenness of external effects means that market prices generally misestimate true social costs and benefits leading to a general misallocation of resources. (For one source see Hunt 1973.)

2. Since people are more interactive with their economic institutions than neoclassical theory admits, the biases introduced in the terms of availability of different goods and services in market economies are magnified over time as people learn to adjust to those biases. That is, to a considerable degree, to be able to get on without constant frustration, we mold our preferences to fit the circumstances we find ourselves in. (For one source see theorem 6.6 in Hahnel and Albert, 1990.)

3. Points 1 and 2 combine to imply that free market systems do not get prices "right." In fact, they get most prices "wrong," and get important ones wrong by a considerable margin. This implies a significant and general misallocation of resources in market economies (See theorem 7.2 in Hahnel and Albert, 1990)–a conclusion directly at odds with the view long held by mainstream economists (now echoed with no further argument by advocates of "market socialism") that whatever else one may like or dislike about markets, at least they yield allocative efficiency. But there are further reasons for doubting that markets yield allocative efficiency. The above criticisms were not the basis for the widespread opposition to markets on efficiency grounds among socialists and political economists that existed until recently. Until recently many critics of capitalism argued that:

4. Market competition unavoidably leads to oligopoly with consequent inefficiencies. And

5. Inefficient business cycles and sectoral imbalances could only be partially alleviated by stabilization policies. It is

ironic that from the 1930s through the 1970s when significant progress was made in the theory and practice of stabilization policies and indicative planning, political economists held firm to their conviction that market disequilibrium was a serious, perhaps fatal flaw. But during the late 1980s and early 1990s when there has been little if any theoretical or empirical work that even purports to shed new light on these subjects and the inefficiencies resulting from market disequilibria have increased dramatically, a majority of political economists have altered their assessment substantially. Suddenly, problems that were once deemed serious are now considered insignificant on the basis of no new evidence! Of course, we are not suggesting there are no reasons for the about-face. The dramatic, recent increase in the political and ideological hegemony of pro-market forces is obvious to all, as is the demise of what was widely assumed to be the only alternative to market allocations. But neither of these changes has any logical bearing on the degree to which market allocations are, in fact, inefficient due to non-competitive structures and disequilibrium dynamics. They have bearing only on ideological reasons, or professional reasons, or perhaps, arguably, political reasons, for holding views—not on evidentiary or analytic reasons.

Pat Devine poses the challenge to market efficiency based on points 4 and 5 as follows: "My overall conclusion is that models of 'market socialism' represent an attempt to square the circle. 'Market socialism' is advocated because markets are alleged to be efficient in generating information and motivating enterprises to act on the basis of that information.... However, the British school of "market socialism" is understandably reluctant to accept this logic, for two basic reasons. First, there is the recognition that atomistic decision-making with respect to investment necessarily involves market uncertainty.... This is what underlies the argument for indicative planning and industrial policy as ways of seeking to reduce market uncertainty without limiting enterprise independence. Yet, unless enterprise independence is limited, market uncertainty cannot be overcome. The second reason for reluctance to accept the logic of efficiency through the market is the desire to allow wider social considerations than those determining enterprise profitability to influence enterprise decision-making.... If wider social considerations are to be taken into account, either the independence of the enterprise to pursue profit maximization must be limited, or the enterprise must be constituted in a way that directly involves representatives of social interests in the decision-making process." (Devine, 1992, page 76) In our view, Devine is right. Enterprise independence and the profit criterion are hallmarks of market systems. Moreover, once one admits that efficiency requires abandoning these features, it is hard to maintain support for the efficiency of market economies since these features are the basis for claims to the efficiency of markets in the first place!

Finally, Chris Tilly typifies the understandable, but illogical recent turnabout of many political economists: "I can recite a list of reasons why capitalist markets don't work: They feed boom-and-bust cycles, fail to provide needed goods such as clean air, and waste economic resources in ways ranging from unemployment to advertising expenditures. But before consigning markets to the dustbin of history, consider a friend's visit to a store selling government-subsidized goods in revolutionary Nicaragua in 1987. The only goods on the shelves were sanitary napkins and Lenin's collected works.... Let's face it: We need markets of some kind. Markets do not ensure that everybody gets enough rice to survive, but they do a good job of matching up needs with suppliers in complex modern economies." (Tilly, 1992, page 6) We're sorry, but markets are no better (or worse) at allocating resources efficiently in Peru or the United States than they were before the demise of communism and the second coming of Monsieur "laissez faire" as the world's Savior.

CRITICISMS OF PARTICIPATORY ECONOMICS

Surprisingly, few if any critics have claimed that participatory economics is infeasible, that is, unlikely to work as we say. Instead, the focus of criticism has been on whether or not it is desirable: a system people would want to live and work in. Here we would like to address the doubts critics have expressed.

UNFREE

Many critics of participatory economics claim that it sacrifices personal freedom to attain other, in their view, less important, ends. Weisskopf argues, for example: "The issue is how much value we should attach to the opportunity for individuals to exercise such libertarian rights as freedom of choice, privacy, and the development of one's own specialized talents and abilities—as compared to the more traditional socialist goals of equity, democracy and solidarity." (Weisskopf 1992, page 21) For Weisskopf, therefore, the debate between participatory economies and "market socialism" largely reduces to a debate over the relative importance of different values. He would have readers believe that while participatory economies may better serve "traditional socialist goals" like equity, democracy, and solidarity, it does so only at the expense of "libertarian values" such as individual freedom and privacy, which in his view are better served by market systems. We find the charge that participatory economics sacrifices libertarian values to be entirely without basis, deriving from a shallow and indefensible interpretation of libertarianism and a biased reading of what composes participatory economics. So, for reasons we clarify below, we reject framing the debate as a choice between worthy values and we reject Weisskopf's conclusion based on that assumption: "Participatory economies best serves one set of 'high principles,' while market socialism best serves a different set of equally 'high principles.' But market socialism is less ambitious, closer to what we already have, and therefore more easily achievable." (Weisskopf 1992, page 22)

But what is a libertarian economy? If people are restricted, for example, from buying another human being, is an economy thereby made less libertarian? Surely there are circumstances that would lead people knowingly and willingly to sell themselves into slavery, yet few would refuse to call an economy libertarian because slavery was outlawed. Likewise, if people are restricted from hiring the services of another human being for a wage, is an economy thereby made less libertarian? There are familiar circumstances that lead people knowingly and willingly to accept what "traditional socialists" called "wage slavery." Does this mean that Weisskopf's model of "market socialism," is not libertarian because the employer-employee relationship is outlawed? To equate libertarianism with freedom of individuals to do whatever they please is a shallow interpretation that robs libertarianism of merit it richly deserves.

It is of course a good thing for people to be free to do what they please—at least, insofar as what they choose to do does not infringe on more important freedoms or rights of others. I should not be free to kill you because that would be robbing you of a more fundamental freedom to live. I should not be free to own you because that robs you of a more fundamental freedom to live your own life. I should not be free to employ you because that robs you of a more fundamental freedom to manage your own laboring capacities. I should not be free to bequeath substantial inheritance to my children because that robs the children of less wealthy parents of their more fundamental right to an equal opportunity in life. Presumably, there is little disagreement about any of this between advocates of "market socialism" and proponents of participatory economies. But are there additional fundamental freedoms and rights that others should not be free to violate in choosing to do what they please? And is one difference between "market socialism" and participatory economics that participatory economies unjustifiably curtail important personal freedoms that markets respect, or that markets violate valid rights participatory economies protect?

Advocates of participatory economics think everyone should have equal opportunity to participate in making economic decisions in proportion to the degree they are affected. We think, in fact, that this is the only way to interpret what "economic freedom" means without having one person's freedom conflict with another's, and we call this goal economic "self-management." We think economic self-management, in precisely this sense, is a fundamental right, so that allowing people freedom to do what they want must not permit them to infringe on others' right to self-management. In other words, we do not think some people should be free to have disproportionate decision making power, leaving others with less. In more familiar terms, we do not think some should be "free" to oppress others with their greater economic power. But we do not think ourselves any less libertarian for wanting to outlaw this type of oppression, any more than abolitionists thought themselves less libertarian for fighting to outlaw slavery.

Advocates of participatory economics also think distributing the burdens and benefits of economic activity fairly, or equitably, means people should benefit in proportion to their effort or personal sacrifice. So we believe economic justice requires that nobody be "free" to appropriate more goods and services than warranted by their personal sacrifice. In more familiar terms, we do not think some should be "free" to exploit others. And, again, we do not think ourselves any less libertarian for wanting to outlaw exploitation, any more than progressives thought themselves less libertarian for fighting for progressive income taxation in the early twentieth century (curtailing the right of folks to keep all income they "earned").

But does this take all the fun out of freedom? If freedom does not include the freedom to oppress and exploit others, what is left? Is a "politically correct" economy—one free from oppression and exploitation—a drab and regimented world, as critics seem to believe? We see no reason to think so. People in a participatory economy are free to develop and pursue preferences for any goods and services they wish. They are free to choose more consumption and less leisure, or visa versa. They are free to distribute their effort and consumption over their lives any way they want. They are free to apply to work wherever they want, free to apply for any job complex at their work place they want, and free to organize a new enterprises to produce whatever they want, however they want, with whomever they want. People are free to educate themselves in any career they want and train for any tasks they want. They're just not free to do any of these things in ways that oppress or exploit others.

Suppose I'm intellectually gifted, score high on standardized tests, do well in my undergraduate studies, am admitted to medical school, and follow with a specialty in brain surgery. Shouldn't I be free to sell my talents or skills to whomever I wish? In a free market economy there would be others willing to pay me up to the value of my contribution. But if this is permitted, there will be others who receive less than the effort, or sacrifice, they incur. There is no way around it. If some receive more than their efforts warrant, others will receive less than their efforts warrant. Those who receive less than their efforts warrant will do so because others receive more than their efforts warrant. And this means those who receive more than their efforts warrant are exploiting those who receive less than their efforts warrant.

Or, suppose I'm particularly competent and energetic and more than willing to spend all my work time analyzing and evaluating different options for my workers' council. Shouldn't I be free to work in a job complex where I am engaged full-time in analytical and decision-making activities? But if I am permitted to work at a job complex significantly more empowering than others, before long my co-workers' formally equal opportunities to participate in economic self-management will not be effectively equal to mine.

What appear to be simple desires for "personal freedom" are not always so simple. But there is another way to see the logic of participatory economics: from the bottom up. The first priority is to guarantee economic justice for those who have never enjoyed it by making sure that people's consumption is commensurate with their sacrifices and by making sure that people's work experience equips them to participate in economic decision making should they want to. And there is also another way to look at talent and education. A participatory economy encourages people to use their talents. In a participatory economy esteem and social recognition for outstanding abilities that create great social benefits for others will be very high. The idea is not to keep people from using their talent or education. But there is no material reward for anything other than effort and sacrifice—since to do otherwise would be inequitable. And while those with greater talent and education may spend part of their work time analyzing complicated consequences, and may have their opinions more highly regarded than others because historically their opinions have been more accurate, they do not get greater decision making *authority* in a participatory economy because this would infringe on the self-management rights of others.

We wish to emphasize that personal freedoms are not sacrificed in the interest of solidarity or community in a participatory economy. This concern, voiced by advocates of markets, has no basis. Only protecting the freedoms of others and the dictates of justice limit the freedoms individuals enjoy in a participatory economy. And in our view limiting one individual's personal freedom or rights because they infringe on the more important freedoms or rights of others is perfectly consistent with the only kind of libertarianism that can be justified.

So how do we answer specific criticisms that participatory economies are "unfree?" For example, "Wouldn't a participatory economic system tend to be too intrusive in restricting individuality, privacy, and freedom of choice?" (Weisskopf 1992, page 18) And: "The more weight one places on … individuality, privacy, and freedom of choice … the more skeptical one will be about the desirability of participatory socialism." (Weisskopf 1992, page 20)

In fact, there simply are no restrictions on individuality or privacy in participatory economics. Anyone who wishes to submit anonymous consumption proposals and avoid feedback from neighbors about the content of their consumption requests is free to do so. Many people have reasonably good relations with their neighbors and would appreciate helpful suggestions. But if this is not the case, in a participatory economy privacy in consumption is available with no questions asked. We see no reason to think that other privacy issues are any less tractable in a participatory economy than any other. Regarding freedom of choice, as explained above, it is restricted only when it infringes on the freedom of choice of others and only in ways that distribute decision-making authority in proportion to the degree people are affected.

Weisskopf says: "Freedom of choice—in how to live, what to consume, what kind of work to do, how to express oneself, how to define one's social identity, etc.—is an important value." (Weisskopf 1992, page 19) Exactly. And there is complete freedom of choice in where and how to live, what to consume, how to express oneself, and how to define one's social identity in a participatory economy. Presumptions to the contrary are unfounded. And the restrictions on what kind of work people do—that job complexes be balanced for empowerment—are only those necessary to ensure everyone's right to economic self-management.

And Weisskopf says: "A participatory system is likely to require people to justify many of their choices ... to some kind of collective decision-making body, which in turn is bound to limit the extent to which people can really get their choices accepted—no matter how democratically decision-making bodies are constituted. By enabling individuals to make most choices without reference to what others think about their decisions, a market system provides much greater freedom of this kind." (Weisskopf 1992, page 19) But, if a participatory economy achieves its goal of self-management—which we understand can only be approximate—then only people affected by decisions will have influence over those decisions, and only to the degree they are affected. If lifestyle, social identity, and what kinds of goods to consume are decisions that only (or predominately) affect an individual—and we agree, for the most part, that they are—then individuals will have control over those decisions in a participatory economy. But there are many decisions some individuals make in a market system that affect other people as well. A participatory economy is designed to provide others affected with influence proportionate to the magnitude of what are "external" effects in a market system. We believe this is only seen as intrusive from the perspective of people accustomed to a market system where people make decisions without reference to the opinion of others even when those others are affected by the outcome. True, factory owners are used to being "free" to pollute the air in market economies and chafe at environmental regulations. Those who make decisions that affect others in market systems are used to being "free" from the opinions and influence of others. But those affected by decisions in a market system who have neither voice nor influence just as surely have their freedom curtailed. The question is not "free" or "unfree" but when unrestricted freedom is legitimate and when it is not.

Weisskopf says: "Many people are likely to prefer doing more specialized work activities than would be permitted under a balanced job complex requirement which means that enforcement of the requirement might well involve implicit or explicit coercion.... Apart from their inhibition of personal freedom, balanced job complexes designed to avoid specialization seem likely to deprive society of the benefits of activities performed well only by people who have devoted a disproportionate amount of time and effort to them." (Weisskopf 1992, page 20) First of all, balanced job complexes are not designed to avoid specialization. They are designed to avoid disparate empowerment and desirability. As already explained, this is to protect the freedom of those who otherwise would not have equal opportunity to participate in economic decision making, and to ensure equity. It is designed to prevent oppression and class divisions. But it does not curtail specialization as usually understood. People will still specialize in brain surgery, electrical engineering, and high voltage welding. But those who perform these more empowering than average tasks will perform less empowering tasks as well. And if the special tasks are more desirable than average, those who perform them will perform some less desirable tasks as well, unless they wish to accept a lower effort rating. We admit this does require training more brain surgeons, electrical engineers, and welders than if none of these specialists ever had to work at any other tasks, assuming, for the sake of discussion, that skilled workers didn't use their advantages to reduce their work time in any event which imposes the same social cost. But this does not mean an end to specialization, nor mean that society will be deprived "of the benefits of activities performed well only by people who have devoted a disproportionate amount of time and effort to them."

Weisskopf says (in a bit of a reversal of course, it seems to us): "Critics of participatory socialism question whether it can adequately protect the legitimate interests of those who hold and wish to act on minority views. True democracy requires not only that people have more or less equal influence over decisions that affect them to the same degree, but that minorities be protected from majority decisions—however equally and fairly arrived at—which disadvantage them in important ways." (Weisskopf 1992, page 18) But advocates of participatory socialism are among the first to recognize the importance of protecting minority views and rights. This is a matter of civil liberties and protection of civil liberties. And while we have not written much on this subject—since we have no particular expertise in constitutional law, civil rights, and civil liberties—we see nothing in the procedures of participatory economies that make protection of minority views or rights more difficult than their protection in other kinds of economies. The only opinion we ever expressed on this matter was to argue for the importance of implementing minority plans for economic projects along with majority plans, whenever possible. We argued this is preferable because it is not only desirable for minorities to allow them to pursue their ideas, it is better for the majority as well, to have contrary opinions tested by their advocates since no majority has ever been right all the time. If there is something specific in the procedures of participatory economies that threatens minority rights and interests we would like very much to hear what it is so it can be reexamined and corrected.

Nancy Folbre says: "The tone of *Looking Forward* sometimes reminds me of a parent telling the kids they can't have any dessert until they've eaten their spinach. Albert and Hahnel sound just as certain that they are right about what's healthy and what's not. They are willing to allow the children to choose different jobs but not to choose specialization and hierarchy. I think many children may feel just as oppressed by this rule as by current structures of constraint that preserve free choice for the privileged few.... Individuals who don't like aspects of their job, specified for them by the larger group, may be as likely to shirk as those who feel that capitalists or coordinators are in control." (Folbre, 1991, page 70) We apologize for our tone if it was condescending. We did not feel at all certain we were right about how best to pursue economic democracy, equity, and solidarity when we published *Looking Forward* and *Participatory Economics*. Instead, we felt the discussion of what constitutes a desirable economy had gotten badly muddled in the context of recent world events. We also felt that a degree of professional-managerial "skin privilege" had intruded into the debate. When working to build a movement dedicated to democracy and justice we can probably all agree that it is critical to examine the possibility of convenient "blind spots." Few engaged in the debate over "market socialism" versus participatory planning have large amounts of private capital they may be tempted to rationalize. There is little need for self-scrutiny on that account. But many of us do enjoy advantages in human capital and empowering, desirable job complexes. In this context, we wished to clarify some issues we find critical and present an alternative to both central planning and "market socialism" that was sufficiently coherent to permit others to evaluate it seriously. And we are gratified that to an extent a serious evaluation has occurred. But that does not bind us to agree with all criticisms. And not agreeing is not the same as claiming omniscience.

Yes, we have presented a case against hierarchical relations of production, as well as a set of procedures to prevent hierarchy from sneaking in the back door after the front door is barred. We do not believe we have thereby prohibited specialization, but we are aware that some aspects of balanced job complexes will not be personally gratifying to those who carry them out. On the other hand there are many aspects of most people's jobs in capitalist or "market socialist" economies that are not gratifying to those who must carry them out, which most assuredly does lead to shirking. But as long as there are unpleasant tasks—and unlike traditional Marxists and modern day high-tech utopians, we believe this will always be the case—someone will have to do them. The difference in a participatory economy from all those that have gone before is not that nobody will ever have to perform a task they dislike, but that any task in anyone's job complex that is not gratifying is there because it would be unfair if it were absent. How much less shirking would take place in an economy where unpleasant tasks are fairly distributed, remains to be seen. But the fact that people can't choose options for themselves that oppress others doesn't seem to us to be an oppressive denial of those people's rights or curtailment of their opportunities any more than denying folks the option to buy slaves or to be a wage slave would be. At the risk of repetition, the issue, as noted earlier, is whether we are talking about removing structures that oppress or structures that liberate. Every pattern of institutions rules out some options and parecon is no exception. But what parecon rules out, it seems to us, is only choices that are oppressive if not to the person making the choice then to other people who endure the implications. It does not rule out choices that are liberating for each person without curtailing other's rights to be equally liberated. Yes, the capitalist confronted with a proposal to eliminate remuneration according to private ownership of means of production will in most cases complain that this curtails his or her freedom to be a wealthy owner. And yes, the coordinator confronted with a proposal to eliminate unbalanced job complexes and authoritarian modes of decision-making will in most cases complain that this curtails his or her freedom to enjoy work of above average comfort and influence. Our reply is, "So what?" The slave owner said the same things about abolition, but that wasn't taken to be a legitimate argument against abolition, of course. What matters is whether we are removing oppressive structures, not whether someone previously enjoying the fruits of oppressive structures would prefer to preserve them.

Weisskopf says: "Certain libertarian objectives associated with personal freedom of choice can best be satisfied only if individuals have the kind of opportunities for choice and for exit that a market system alone can provide." (Weisskopf 1992, page 22) The assumption that "exit" is more difficult in participatory economies than other systems is unfounded. In capitalist economies what can workers do who don't like their boss? In public enterprise market economies what can you do if you don't like your boss or the majority decisions of your work mates? Switching workplaces or starting up a new enterprise is the exit option in any economy. In a participatory economy, workers are free to leave their workplaces and apply for work in any other workplace. And we believe participatory economies' iteration facilitation boards would make finding a new, more compatible work site easier than even social democratic Swedish-style Labor Market Boards. Moreover, convincing an industry federation committee of the social usefulness of a new enterprise is similar to convincing a bank—whether privately or publicly owned—that a new enterprise will prove profitable (though instead of profits being the issue, social value is). As for what you do if you come to dislike your neighbors—if it gets bad enough you move in a participatory economy, just like you do in any other economy. But with your income secure, and consumer facilitation boards for assistance, again, it should be easier.

Insufficient Incentives

When working on the procedures for a participatory economy we assumed the primary concern would be with allocation. After all, we were advocating abandoning both markets and central planning, which most economists presume are the only conceivable ways to determine the social opportunity costs of productive resources in order to allocate them efficiently. In the words of Sam Bowles: "The debate proceeds as if the menu of institutional choices offers just two items: command—meaning centralized planning; and competition—meaning the neoclassical textbook rendition of the market. Our task, one imagines, is to find some judicious combination of these two conceptually homogeneous and unproblematic poles.... But the plan versus market debate reflects an impoverished view of markets and the alternatives to markets, one that thwarts the consideration of the essential political and moral issues: namely, the manner in which markets shape human development and structure the exercise of power. Thus if the economist's first disability is to ignore the non-economic impacts of economic choices, the second is the economist's tendency to assume that the alternative to the invisible hand is Big Brother's fist." (Bowles, 1991, page 11-12) So we assumed this was the major obstacle—demonstrating that a qualitatively new allocation procedure was capable of generating accurate estimates of social opportunity costs and thereby able to allocate resources efficiently.

Predictably, those who practice free market ideology as their religion and presume that only markets can allocate resources efficiently, felt no need to examine the procedures of participatory planning or the analysis we offered. But surprisingly, among those whose faith is less strong, and who examined the procedures of participatory planning, none has challenged our claim that, in theory, participatory planning will yield socially efficient outcomes under less restrictive conditions than market models. Some find participatory planning undesirably cumbersome and time consuming, but no one has claimed it fails to yield efficient outcomes under the assumptions specified.

On the other hand, there has been widespread skepticism about participatory economies' ability to employ scarce human talents and skills efficiently, and to achieve dynamic or motivational efficiency.

REACTIONS TO PARECON • 187

Would balanced job complexes under-employ scarce talents and socially costly training? Would people be motivated to work sufficiently hard? Would efforts be directed toward fulfilling socially desirable needs? Would people be sufficiently motivated to pursue education and training in socially useful careers and skills? Would individuals be sufficiently motivated to search for new innovations? Would workers' councils be adequately motivated to pursue and implement new innovations? Would participatory economies be sufficiently dynamic?

Folbre argues: "Personal endowments as well as preferences differ greatly. Up to a point, specialization provides important efficiency gains. A certain level of specialization and hierarchy lowers transactions and training costs." (Folbre, 1991, page 70) Indeed, specialization does lower training costs. So we agree that requiring those whose training is more socially costly than average to also perform tasks in areas requiring less training incurs extra social costs since it means more people must receive socially costly training. But we pointed out that this efficiency loss needs to be weighed against efficiency gains from *real* worker self-management, better morale among workers, and greater familiarity with the overall work process for all workers. If there are still net efficiency losses, which we find unlikely, these are the price of making self-management real, rather than a hollow sham.

While hierarchy does lower transaction costs, this does not mean that we must tolerate permanent hierarchies. Permanent hierarchies subvert self-management and create class distinctions. But clearly enforced lines of responsibility and authority in workplaces do not require permanent hierarchies. Making sure that workers who exercise managerial authority in one area are subject to authority from others in other areas lowers transaction costs in production just as much as permanent hierarchies do, but without creating social inequities or incurring class differences and associated hostilities and the inefficiencies they in turn introduce.

Alec Nove complains that: "In the absence of a market 'the supplier is usually designated by the supply plan, and is therefore in a position of an absolute monopolist.' The supplier therefore can sacrifice quality to meeting quantity goals, by which fulfillment is measured. 'I can be meaningfully instructed to give fifty lectures, but it is not so easy to enforce an order that I give good lectures.' How can one measure quality except by consumer choice, which negates planned supply, in turn negating plan, and which requires a market?" (Mandel,

1993, page 350 quoting Alec Nove) In fact, in participatory economies consumer councils and federations, answerable only to the consumers they represent, are the recipients of deliveries. We see no reason to believe quality will go uncontested under these circumstances. Negotiations over expectations and quality between consumer and producer federations rather than between individual consumers and suppliers should increase pressure on producers to maintain quality. Is it harder for producers to hoodwink Ralph Nader consumer protection organizations or the average individual citizen? (But, of course, this assumes there is something to be gained by such hoodwinking, which while true in a market economy is false in a participatory economy.)

Weisskopf says: "Wouldn't it be very wasteful to try to allocate labor without an incentive system that rewards individuals according to the market-determined value of their work contributions?" (Weisskopf 1992, page 16) Well, it is true that in participatory economies workers are not "paid" according to the social value of their contributions. Workers are "paid" according to effort expended on the job, because that is what is fair. But the process of participatory planning charges workplaces for workers according to the value of their laboring capacities in their most socially useful and efficient employment. And since participatory planning is the procedure for allocating labor in a participatory economy, Weisskopf's concern does not apply to a participatory economy. Yes, in market economies allocating labor efficiently requires paying people "according to the market-determined value of their work contributions," which means market systems must pay people unfairly. But participatory economies have been designed precisely so we can have our cake and eat it too. People are compensated fairly—wages based on effort—but labor is allocated according to productivity—users are charged true social opportunity costs.

Mark Hagar argues: "Because success, even in a non-capitalist order, may easily turn on talent, luck, and other morally undeserved factors, it is easy for the authors to show that equity favors distribution according to effort. My question, however, is whether they succeed in showing that distribution according to effort achieves efficiency alongside equity.... A society seeking optimum production needs to discourage clumsy effort and encourage proficient effort so as to avoid waste. Otherwise, the less successful have no material incentive to modify bungling methods or to seek work where their comparative advantage in contribution is greater. For efficiency, one must at least reward efforts to improve the success of efforts, and rewarding contribution may be the only feasible way to do so." (Hagar, 1991, page 71)

And Weisskopf adds: "They [Albert & Hahnel] propose that the consumption opportunities available to individuals be linked to an individual's input into the production process—in the form of personal effort made or personal sacrifice endured ... Albert & Hahnel's proposal would surely lead to greater equity in the reward for labor than the market-based alternative, but their claim of greater efficiency is misguided.... First of all, it is very difficult to observe and measure an individual's sacrifice or work effort.... Any input-oriented incentive scheme would tend to encourage the substitution of quantity for quality of effort. Moreover, people would have an interest in understating their natural talents and abilities.... Second ... [while] it would presumably elicit greater work effort and sacrifice on the part of individuals, it would do nothing to assure that such effort and sacrifice were expended in a desirable way. The social good is best served by encouraging activities the results of which are highly valued relative to the cost of undertaking those activities. In order to motivate people to expend their efforts in a desirable way, it is therefore necessary to reward activities according to the value of work output rather than according to the quantity of work input." (Weisskopf 1992, page 16-17)

Hagar and Weisskopf make an important point here. It is a different point than the previous concern with allocating labor to its most productive use. Here the issue is whether people who are rewarded for effort and sacrifice will be motivated to expend their efforts in socially desirable ways rather than clumsily. For example, will they work to produce more, rather than better?

In market economies a single incentive is used to motivate both quantity and quality of effort and to direct effort in socially desirable ways—material rewards for the value of outcome. But rewarding the value of outcome does not just reward these three things. It also rewards talent and luck—luck in what job one occupies and with what equipment and work mates one works, luck in whether applied effort yields smaller or greater output, and luck in one's own, or someone else's guess about what others find socially useful. So market economies do not reward only the things that efficiency requires. They reward those things, and other things as well.

Participatory economies use three different incentives to reward quantity of effort, proficiency of effort, and socially useful application of effort, in slightly different proportions. There are material rewards for quantity of effort. Proficiency of effort is motivated in enterprises by the incentives in participatory planning for enterprises to increase the ratio of the social benefit of outputs to the social cost of inputs (SC/SB), and within enterprises by the interests of coworkers and the supervisory system to motivate proficiency in each worker because lack of proficiency in one requires greater effort from others. Thus, peer pressure from those inside and outside one's workplace is important in motivating proficiency. Socially useful application in training and work effort is primarily motivated in participatory economies by social esteem and recognition. I maximize my chance for social esteem if I educate and train myself in areas that are my comparative advantage and if I orient my efforts toward maximizing the social benefit of what I do.

But it is important to bear in mind who is doing the monitoring, rating, and evaluating in a participatory economy. My work mates and I decide how our work will be monitored. My work mates judge my efforts. And social recognition comes from my work mates, other workers in the same federation, and from consumers through their consumer federations. It is easy to point out that maximizing effort input is not really what we want to motivate. Weisskopf is right that we want to maximize the social value that results from a given human effort. But when we talked of rewarding effort rather than outcome, we meant effort expended proficiently to socially useful ends. And in a participatory economy that is the only kind of effort it makes any sense for one's fellow workers to try and reward in either supervision or effort ratings. Why would my fellow work mates give me high effort ratings for taking two hours longer to mop rooms because I mopped from the door to the far wall and had to mop over my foot prints as I left? Why would my fellow workers give me high ratings because I worked four hours to copyedit a piece because I didn't use the spell checker and grammar checker? We think many of the problems Weisskopf and Hagar foresee stem from misconstruing what we meant by "effort" and disappear in the context of who is doing the judging.

It is also important to keep in mind who is judging when thinking about measurement problems. Of course there are problems measuring effort—just as there are problems measuring the value of output and attributing that value to different people involved. In a participatory economy effort rating committees in different workplaces can put as much or as little time into measuring effort as they wish. And they can collect whatever information they wish—hours worked, indications of output, improvement, comparisons with other enterprises, self-evaluation, or evaluation of team members. Nothing is perfect. To the extent they measure inaccurately, there will be inequities in effort ratings. But we have a hard time believing those inequities would not be considerably less than the inequities built into the normal, successful operations of "market socialist" or capitalist economies. (It is important to realize that payment according to effort and sacrifice in a parecon is accompanied, as well, by working at balanced job complexes. If people do their job, so to speak, then due to the fact that their job complex is average, they are working at society's norm, and remunerated accordingly. The only real on-going measurement is periodic reassessment of job complex definitions, and attention to over time or reduced work time, and to the intransigent case of workers who just aren't fulfilling their responsibilities.)

In participatory economies there are both material and social incentives, and both kinds of incentives can be used to motivate proficient work effort, socially useful training and education, and innovation in product design and production technique. But every attempt is made to maximize the use of peer pressure and social esteem. And there is relatively greater reliance on social incentives to motivate socially useful education, training, and innovation, and relatively greater reliance on material incentives to motivate work effort. The reason for the first choice is obvious to any parent who has tried to minimize the use of allowances to get children to do their chores. The reasons for the second choice are: Greater material rewards for greater sacrifice is equitable, greater material rewards for education or innovation is usually not; and contributions that come from innovation and education are usually owed to a diffuse network of people rather than a single individual.

We also believe that while those pursuing education in more socially valuable careers could be rewarded with greater consumption rights as an incentive, it should seldom be necessary to do so since the social and personal cost of the training is born by society rather than the individual, it is not unusual to like to study what you are good at, and chances of earning greater social esteem are better if one trains in one's comparative advantage. In any case, if someone who would have been an excellent surgeon decides not to pursue graduate studies (thereby exercising their right to predominantly impact decisions over their own life course and thereby attain a desirable rather than depressing outcome for themselves), we have no doubt there will be many other talented people in any parecon society who will accept admission to medical school. (This point seems to escape many of our critics who by their comments think instead that the pool of potential surgical talent for a parecon corresponds quite closely to the pool of actual surgeons in a capitalist economy, rather than extending far into other cultural groups, genders, and classes than those now monopolizing skilled and conceptual positions—and similarly for other conceptual and skilled positions).

Stimulating innovations is somewhat different. Most innovations are the result of cumulative human efforts with a good deal of luck involved, and this provides good reason for not awarding an individual who puts the finishing touch on a cumulative advance with substantial material rewards. That is why we think efforts to minimize material rewards for innovation are warranted, and why we suggest stimulating innovation directly through planned expenditures on research and development under the management of consumer and producer federations, and social esteem and recognition for both individuals and enterprises that are particularly innovative. But should it prove a good idea, participatory planning can award innovative enterprises with job complexes that are more desirable than average or with consumption allowances that are higher than average for specified periods of time. And this can be done, moreover, without retarding the spread of the innovation to other enterprises (the deleterious side-effect of market incentives to innovate). If the citizens in a participatory economy decided in a democratic dialogue that their economy was insufficiently dynamic, material incentives such as these could certainly be deployed. We think, however, that very few, if any, material rewards for innovation would prove necessary, except perhaps in early phases of a participatory economy, and we believe there are good reasons to work particularly hard to hold them to a minimum.

CYBERNETIC OVERLOAD

Weisskopf says: "Wouldn't the allocation of resources in a complex economy by means of participatory decision-making institutions place impossible demands on information processing and inordinate demands on people's time?" (Weisskopf 1992, page 13)

And he adds: "The mere listing of [the requirements for decision-making in a participatory economy] is enough to generate skepticism about whether and how they can possibly be met. Even if, in principle, institutions and processes can be developed to accomplish the necessary tasks (and Albert & Hahnel and Devine have advanced some ingenious ideas to do so), one is bound to wonder whether the whole system would actually function in practice. Assuming that computer technology could be relied upon to process and disseminate the enormous amount of information needed to make the system work, how would people be persuaded to provide the needed information in an unbiased and disinterested manner? And even if all the needed information could be accurately compiled, wouldn't participatory planning require each individual to dedicate so much time, interest and energy to assessing the information and participating in decision-making meetings that most people would get sick and tired of doing it?" (Weisskopf 1992, page 14-15)

In defining participatory economic institutions, we paid close attention to the incentives for people to provide needed information truthfully. It is in the interest of any person who wants to win approval for a consumption request or production proposal to provide qualitative information explaining why the quantitative estimates based on estimated social opportunity costs fail to account for some particular circumstances. As to whether people would go overboard and exaggerate needs and disabilities, perhaps they will. But such accounts are only testimony others will review when deciding if exceptions should be granted, and presumably people will learn to evaluate such qualitative information with a critical eye. Regarding the quantitative information and genesis of our indicative prices, we are familiar with the literature on incentive compatibility and believe we have designed an incentive compatible mechanism. Participatory planning is completely different from central planning where individual producers have incentives to hide their true capabilities from planning authorities.

Weisskopf wonders: "Isn't the process of democratic decision-making sufficiently complex and problematic that it should be applied only to a limited range of critical decision-making areas?" (Weisskopf 1992, page 15) And adds, "Isn't the practice of participatory democracy sufficiently difficult, time-consuming and emotionally draining that it would in practice have to be limited to a relatively small range of decisions?" (Weisskopf 1992, page 15) As well as: "These kinds of concerns about the operation of democratic decision-making processes should not of course be read as a condemnation of democracy.... Rather, such concerns suggest that democratic political institutions ought to focus on a critical and manageable range of decision-making areas, rather than be used for all kinds of economic as well as political decisions." (Weisskopf 1992, page 15-16)

This sounds reasonable, at first listening. And it is certainly true that we should devote more decision-making time to more important decisions and less to less important ones. But people should have decision-making input in all decisions to the degree they are affected. And people, themselves, should decide which decisions are of little importance and therefore those on which *they* do not wish to spend much time. In fact, many of the decisions that people care a great deal about are ones concerning their own neighborhood and workplace— so spending time on these issues is not unwarranted. But excluding people from a say over long-term national investment plans is also undesirable. In participatory economies people are free not to attend meetings, or to call for closure, or to leave meetings early as they desire. But this is not the same as saying some issues are too small to warrant democracy, or that some issues are too complex and distant for people to decide for themselves. Any time a decision is not worth spending any more time over, people are free to call a halt to the debate, vote, and move on. But democratic decision making is a process that is more likely to occur efficiently and with good result the more it is practiced wherever people have an interest.

Weisskopf asks: "Won't the politicization of all kinds of decisions lead to excessive conflict, strife, and anger?" (Weisskopf 1992, page 15) Market systems are clever at disguising exploitation and oppression. Painful consequences often seem to be the result of market competition that none can forestall, and we are taught that market competition is socially beneficial. In market economies the distribution of inequity is largely impersonal, which is an important reason the inequities have been tolerated so long. Participatory economies, in contrast, make every attempt to make the consequences of individual and group choices for others as graphic and plain as possible—because otherwise people cannot engage in knowledgeable, collective self-management. So, we plead guilty to politicizing economic choices, but with cause. If you get a low effort rating you will know it is because your fellow workers thought that's all you deserved. If your enterprise's proposal is not accepted, you will know it is because other workers' councils thought it was inefficient or too lazy. If your consumption proposal is rejected, you will know your neighbors did not think your work effort rating merited consuming that much, or that your special needs requests were not compelling. However, we do not believe participatory economies will lead to the kind of conflict, strife, and anger that plague private enterprise and market economies. By providing an open, democratic, efficient, and fair procedure for negotiating conflicts of interest, we feel participatory planning minimizes the probability of strife and anger after the plan has been agreed to. More to the point, be eliminating structural conflicts of interest and particularly class conflicts and difference, parecon removes by far the largest source of continuous conflict and strife.

Folbre complains: "One perverse incentive could be labeled 'The Dictatorship of the Sociable.' Some people really like meetings. They like to talk, to negotiate, to debate. As a result, they often attend meetings enthusiastically, and they often prevail at them." (Folbre, 1991, page 69) And Weisskopf adds: "In practice such a system might well enable some people to exercise much greater influence over decisions than others. Disproportionate influence would not arise from disproportionate wealth or income, but from disproportionate interest in and aptitude for the relevant decision-making processes." (Weisskopf 1992, page 15)

We should be frank. Long live the dictatorship of the sociable if that is the only alternative to the dictatorship of the wealthy or the dictatorship of the better educated—which is what capitalism and "market socialism" come down to. But isn't it ironic that those who worry about the dictatorship of the sociable are the same people who find balancing job complexes—which is done precisely to guarantee equal opportunity to participate effectively for all and equal impact of work on our skills and knowledge relevant to participating in decision-making meetings—unjustifiable infringements on personal freedom? The purpose of balancing for empowerment is to prevent the economic system from generating unequal endowments of what we might call "social capital" that effectively disenfranchise significant segments of the workforce. Balancing for empowerment is the only way to preclude a "dictatorship of the educated and managerial," who needn't be all that sociable! And it goes a long ways, it seems to us, to also prevent any kind of sociability advantage, which in practice isn't really a taste for meetings, as suggested, but rather, again, a set of skills and talents for expressing oneself and influencing others at meetings that in turn make meetings less onerous.

Folbre adds: "A related problem is the "Let's Not Piss Anybody Off" principle…. Many individuals would rather accept some decline in collective efficiency rather than risk their social reputation as a nice person. Nobody wants to be seen as a hard-ass. So discipline is weak. Individuals who fail to do what they promised to do are not sanctioned. Individuals who always do what they promise to do are ripped off." (Folbre, 1991, page 69) Enterprises in a participatory economy that indulge in this kind of "liberalism" will have a difficult time achieving an acceptable ratio of social benefits of product to social costs of inputs. If the hard-working nice people Folbre is so concerned about want to carry their irresponsible work mates, they may choose to do so rather than struggling with them. But participatory planning and effort ratings are "incentive compatible" in the sense that people who engage in this kind of liberalism "pay a price."

We freely admit that most people would spend more time in workplace meetings in a participatory economy than a hierarchical one. But this is because most people are excluded from workplace decision-making in hierarchical economies. And we also freely admit that democratic decision-making takes more "meeting time" than autocratic decision-making. Having everyone get vacations, not just a few; or having everyone get work breaks, not just a few; or having everyone get weekends off, not just a few, also reduces output. In all cases the issue is whether the lost output is worth it. In any case, we should note that decisions arrived at democratically should take far less time to enforce than ones arrived at autocratically.

But further, we also think critics have failed to appreciate an important feature of participatory planning when criticizing the amount of meeting time our social, iterative planning process would require. For the most part people and their delegated representatives do not meet face to fact to discuss and negotiate how to coordinate their activities, as critics seem to assume. Instead, individuals and councils submit proposals for their own activities, receive new estimates of social costs, and submit revised proposals. Moreover, rather than have delegates from federations meet to hammer out the "end game" of the planning process, we proposed that after a number of iterations had defined the basic contours of the plan, the professional staffs of iteration facilitation boards would define a few feasible plans within those contours for constituents to vote on without ever meeting and debating. We also did not propose face to face meetings where different groups plead their cases for consumption or production proposals that did not meet normal quantitative standards. Instead we proposed that councils submit qualitative information as part of their proposals, so that higher level federations could grant exceptions should they choose to. And the procedure for disapproving proposals is a simple up or down vote of federation members, rather than a rancorous meeting. Finally, to actually assess the "meeting implications" or "time implications" more generally of participatory economics, one has to not only consider the meeting or time requirements added but also those removed (due to elimination of various hostilities and practices, etc.), something we did in some detail in the books presenting the model, but which critics entirely ignore.

WE ARE HOMO ECONOMUS NOT HOMO SOCIALIS

Weisskopf worries: "Wouldn't a participatory economic system be viable only if there were a prior transformation of people's basic consciousness from one that is individually oriented to one that is socially oriented?" (Weisskopf 1992, page 17)

And adds: "In order for mechanisms [of participatory economics] to add up to a workable system of motivation which could substitute for individual material incentives, there would surely have to be a wholesale conversion of human behavior patterns from homo economus to what might best be characterized as homo socialis—i.e. a person whose very consciousness was socially rather than individually oriented." (Weisskopf 1992, page 18)

He argues: "The first issue is whether and how people could be expected to change from homo economus, as we know him/her in contemporary capitalist societies, to homo socialis, as he/she is depicted in the operation of participatory socialist societies.... If people act essentially as homo economus, it follows that a significant amount of inequality, hierarchy, competition, etc. is a necessary ingredient of an efficient economic system." (Weisskopf 1992, page 21)

Finally: "To transform homo economus into homo socialis would thus involve a massive change in people's mind-sets. Such a transformation might conceivably be imposed on a society by an authoritarian élite, but it is virtually impossible to imagine it being generated by a democratic process that respected the current attitudes and preferences of the general public." (Weisskopf 1992, page 21-22)

Concerns such as these—that a participatory economy assumes people are altruists, or that a participatory economy requires a different set of human motivations than those people have currently and that there is no way to get from here to there—are usually the last line of argument against pursuing participatory economics as a political project. Weisskopf poses the essential dilemma of *all* fundamental social change well when he asks how fundamental human and social change can be compatible with democracy.

We are under no illusions that a democratic economy cannot result from a non-democratic political process. Only a social movement committed to democracy and justice in all spheres of social life, supported "body and soul" by at least a third of the population, and approved of by at least another third of the population, could possibly establish a participatory economy. That means that a third of the population would have to be convinced that they wanted an economy that was compatible with homo socialis rather than reproductive of homo economus. And it means that the solid beginnings of such a system of motivation and reward would have to be well established during decades of struggle—which places important conditions on the internal dynamics such a movement requires. But this is precisely the democratic process that can lead to a participatory economy. Those who are sufficiently disgusted and or oppressed by the results of the economies of greed to struggle for a just economy of cooperation and to engage in that struggle respecting the principles they are fighting for will establish the "living proof" of the possibility and advantages of an economy based on those principles. That is also presumably how they could win the approval of another third of the population. We always assumed a transition could require many decades of blood, sweat, and tears with no guarantees. But, for us, that is a better prospect than another five hundred years of solitude, with present results guaranteed, or, far more likely if we continue as is, some form of catastrophic ecological or social collapse.

But notice that the third of the population that is the movement for social change does not impose a participatory economy on the rest of the population. Only when there is another third that votes along with the diehards to take the plunge, would a democratically elected government have a mandate to set up a participatory economy.

But when this occurs, in our hypothetical scenario, there will still be one third of the population who neither believe in nor support many of the features of a participatory economy. And there will be more than one third who are acclimated only to incentives reproductive of homo economus. Moreover, few in the group who have been exposed to different incentives through participation in a democratic, equitable movement will have both feet firmly in the psychological world of the "new man and woman." But we are under no illusions about this either, which is why the features of a participatory economy are designed *not to assume* homo socialis, but to work with people who are homo economus and to help transform most of them, over time, into homo socialis.

Unless we are interested in an economy suited only to saints, a participatory economy must have mechanisms that *pressure* people to behave in socially responsible ways, making such behavior the wise course regardless of one's holdover individualist or even anti-social inclinations. The principle mechanism that compels workers' and consumers' councils to behave in a socially responsible way is peer pressure. Workers' councils must demonstrate that their proposals generate an acceptable excess of social benefits over social costs. And consumers' councils must demonstrate that the social cost of the goods they request is consistent with the work effort ratings of their members. Ultimately, if self-imposed social responsibility as well as peer pressure fail to yield socially responsible behavior, a suitably defined majority of other councils imposes an acceptable proposal. The principle mechanism that compels individually responsible behavior are effort ratings by one's work mates and consumption allocations based on effort ratings as well as need. The logic here is to run the economy in a way that ensures that even homo economi will behave as homo socialis. The idea is that practice makes perfect, not that any of us are, or ever will be, one hundred percent homo socialis. We are not surprised that people who are drawn to participatory economies have a spasmodic, confessional reaction. As one student put it, "I believe that people, myself included, want to, on some occasions, think only of themselves." Participatory economies are not unmindful of this aspect of the human condition, despite what critics have assumed.

Consider this example. You work in a publishing house and propose an innovation there as an investment. It will make work relations and tasks a little more pleasant while publishing new titles. Across town, or across the country, those working in a mine also propose an innovation. It will make conditions dramatically better for those mining coal. Homo economi (motivated solely by self) in the publishing house, you, say, is concerned only with the conditions he or she will have when the economic period unfolds, not with those the miners will have. Homo-socialis in the publishing house cares about self and others. Our critics seem to think that for a parecon to work everyone has to be homo-socialis, thinking always about themselves and others, otherwise investments that have the greatest possible value won't be chosen. But this is false. In parecon, instead, even the narrowly self-oriented person in the publishing house has a greater interest in the investment in the mine being implemented than in the investment in the publishing house being implemented. For we all have balanced job complexes and what benefits each is that the social average job complex across the whole society be improved as much as possible, not that a lesser innovation occur in our own place of work rather than a greater one elsewhere. Quality of life for me, with a balanced job complex including publishing, etc., is more enhanced by innovation that eliminates horrid mining conditions than by one that has less dramatic impact on already above average publishing conditions. The point is simple. In parecon the interest of each is the enhancement of all, because the enhancement of each depends on the enhancement of all. Some will have true empathy, more and more over time. But even without it, the choice to make is the same.

Incidentally, a concern for the compatibility of consciousness and institutions is why we cannot accept the olive branch from "market socialists" who are kind enough to offer it: "Even if one's ultimate hope is to progress to a participatory form of socialist society, a gradual move to some form of 'market socialism,' which would begin to change people's actual socioeconomic environment in a more socialist direction, would appear to be a necessary first step in achieving a democratic transition." (Weisskopf 1992, page 22) The abstract idea is fine;

the problem is that the logic of "market socialism" is precisely a socio-economic environment conducive to the reproduction of homo economus and the eradication of homo socialis! Throughout this book we have put the label market socialism in quote markets precisely because there is nothing particularly socialist about it, beyond the eliination of private ownership, which would be a constant threat to return in any event. If people have both potentials—to be greedy, self centered homo economus and empathetic, outgoing, homo socialis—and if the principle obstacle to a transition to a participatory economy is a long history of reinforcing the former and repressing the latter, how can an economy that continues to do just that be an important part of a transition strategy? True, things would be far easier if it could. But to pretend "market socialism" will lead to participatory economics seems illogical and utopian to us. It is far more likely, as practice has indeed shown, to lead right back to capitalism.

INCAPABLE OF INTERNATIONAL ECONOMIC RELATIONS

One initial criticism of participatory economies was that they could not engage in international economic relations with other kinds of economies. In the April 1993 issue of Z Magazine we gave some tentative suggestions regarding how participatory economies might engage in international economic activities: We said "we should not be too disapproving if a group of historically distinct participatory economies agreed to: trade goods and services at terms that were beneficial to all, but more beneficial to countries with lower levels of consumption per unit of effort; share productive knowledge as quickly as possible with compensation awarded in some cases; and share unequal stocks of productive resources over a reasonable period of time. But even so, this must be arranged through democratic discussion and planning based on moral argument and informed by serious attempts to re-estimate the external costs and benefits of economic activities. Otherwise it would still corrode economic democracy and equity, as well as continue to destroy the planet at an escalating pace."

If a participatory economy engages in trade with hierarchical and exploitative economies that have higher levels of consumption per unit of effort it need only pursue its own advantage in negotiations in order to advance the above principles. On the other hand, if a participatory economy engaged in trade with less materially advanced hierarchical and exploitative economies, equity would require the participatory economy to give its international economic partners a majority of the mutual benefits. To do otherwise would seriously undermine the values and principles necessary to the functioning of a participatory economy.

While critics have not had time to react to our tentative suggestions on this score, we find it comforting that the conclusions we came to were consistent with the conclusions of the Non-Aligned Movement during the debate over a New International Economic Order in the North South debate in the late 1970s, as well as more recent recommendations from progressive circles in the aftermath of NAFTA and GATT. [See Jeremy Brecher, "After NAFTA: Global Village or Global Pillage?" (*Nation*, December 6 1993), and Cavanagh, Broad and Weiss, "Global New Deal" (*Nation*, December 27 1993).] One additional complication we see for a materially advanced participatory economy is what to do if the effects of a generous distribution of the benefits of international cooperation to an economy that was internally hierarchical and exploitative was counter-productive to democratic and egalitarian reforms within that economy. Our inclination is that representatives of the reform movement within the exploitative economy should decide if the participatory economy should engage in trade with their economy, and if so, on what terms. This is analogous to letting the ANC decide when other nations should trade with or invest in South Africa as long as it pursues apartheid, and on what terms.

FINAL THOUGHTS

The debate so far has clarified some important issues for participatory economics.

First, in theory, equity does not require balancing job complexes for desirability as long as differences in desirability of work conditions are counterbalanced by unequal consumption claims. In other words, if someone wanted to work a more desirable job complex and was willing to consume less in order to do so, this could, overall, still be equitable. So denying people "freedom" to choose to do this, or "freedom" to work at a less desirable job complex in return for greater consumption privileges, is not required by the dictates of justice or the principles of participatory economics. But there are important practical obstacles. Most important, whether job complexes are balanced for desirability or not, they must be balanced for empowerment to protect self-management. In reality, however, there is often a significant correlation between empowering and desirable tasks. Second, your work mates may not want to work less desirable complexes so that you can work a more desirable one. In other words, one would have to arrange to suit one's preferences in this regard with work mates with compatible preferences. It is therefore possible this would be one important difference between different workplaces one considered in applying for work: some would have job complexes balanced for desirability and others would have job complexes that were more and less desirable than average, with offsetting effort allotments. Of course, real world social and technological conditions could also impinge on the degree of flexibility in this area. Even so, we see no reason to ban flexibility in theory. The essential issue with respect to equity, as compared to empowerment, is only that the *overall* burdens and benefits of work *and* consumption—which is to say economic life as a whole—should be balanced for everyone in the economy.

Second, there are, in fact, some complications that arise if we succeed in rewarding sacrifice, or effort, and do not materially reward talent. For example, imagine a world with capitalist economies, "market socialist" economies, and participatory economies all existing side by side. If there were people in the participatory economy who owned a greater than proportionate share of the physically productive assets in the economy, there would be an incentive for them to emigrate with the capital they own to a capitalist economy. But, of course, nobody owns the physically productive assets in participatory economies, and trying to emigrate with state property would obviously be theft, so this is not a real problem. However, there would be particularly talented people in participatory economies, as there are in all economies. And there would be people who had received substantial amounts of education at social, rather than personal expense. And in each of these cases there would therefore exist a material incentive to emigrate to "market socialist" economies where they would receive greater material reward for the contribution their talent or education permits them to make. If there is no respect and esteem for talent and expertise in the participatory economy, if self-management, equity, and solidarity are not forthcoming, and if people do not come to see talent and socially costly education as a "gift" that confers an obligation to benefit less fortunate citizens who are engaging in equal or greater sacrifices—then the material advantages of emigration may become weighty. We support the "Cuban" rather than the "Russian" policy response. The Cuban government always said "good riddance to bad rubbish—goodbye gusano." Soviet policy was often to restrict emigration of the more highly talented or educated. A logical case could be made for requiring people to pay back the cost of their greater education that was paid for at public expense, but the implication of keeping people "captive" who want to leave is unacceptable, in our view. In any case, a participatory economy with a strong net out migration, or an emigration-immigration pattern that produced a strong brain drain, is not a participatory economy that deserves to withstand the test of time. We would never defend a system that had to put up fences to keep people in. But we remain confident that those who would leave to exploit their talent or education elsewhere would be more than adequately replaced from the pool of talent and education remaining.

We should note, also, that there is an analogous problem that could lead to black markets in a participatory economy. That is, in activities without economies of scale, highly talented or educated individuals could strike mutually beneficial deals with consumers outside the "formal" participatory economy. Instead of working in an official workplace where they would be paid only according to their effort, they could make the product and sell it on the black market for a price under the social opportunity cost—the benefit to the buyer—but high enough to compensate the producer more than they would have received for doing the same work at their official work site, since the "market would bear" a price reflecting their effort and greater than average talent or training. What would minimize this problem—and it is a problem because it leads to inequities and undermines the system of incentives participatory economies rely on—are the considerable economies of scale in production of most goods and services, and the popular consciousness that would see this activity as "unfair." Also, to the extent that material rewards were less important and social rewards more important in achieving esteem, such activity by talented and educated people would be counterproductive.

Third, Weisskopf says: "Advocates of participatory planning ... tend to ignore the myriad problems involved in establishing fair and efficient democratic decision-making processes. First of all, choice among alternative voting conventions is complex and critical: when should decisions be made by simple majority, by a super majority, or by consensus? What will distinguish constitutionally protected rights from those subject to democratic voting?" (Weisskopf 1992, page 15) This point is well taken. While we have gone into considerable detail, we have not been comprehensive regarding the exact procedures for approving and disapproving proposals in participatory planning, the exact types of votes, or steps to take, etc. We continue to believe the general principles are correct—that only when councils can demonstrate that their proposals are socially beneficial and responsible is there reason for others to approve them. But no doubt disagreements will arise, and the modern game theoretic literature regarding voting coalitions may well have contributions to make in this area that require further exploration. Moreover, as we acknowledged earlier, constitutional rights that supersede majority rule are important issues in any society and economy, including a participatory economy. We agree that more work needs to be done in this area, as well as how to relate to people who feel themselves (and are) affected by a decision another would take, but who should perhaps have no legitimate right to influence the decision, nonetheless. A majority of most American communities we lived in would have liked to cut our long hair in the late 1960s since it really galled them. But that doesn't mean that the principle of self-management gives them the right to do it!

As we have said elsewhere: "Ultimately, the social process of consciously, democratically, and equitably coordinating our interconnected economic activities is fundamentally different from the social process of competing against one another in the exchange of goods and services. And while both 'solutions' to the economic problem are feasible, only the former is compatible with self-management (decision making input in proportion to the degree one is affected by the outcome), equity (to each according to personal sacrifice or effort), solidarity (concern for the well-being of others), variety (diversity of outcomes and methodologies), and efficiency (maximizing the social benefits resulting from the use of scarce productive resources), not to speak of ecological sustainability." (Albert and Hahnel, 1992b, page 131) And that is why we need participatory planning, rather than markets.

REFERENCES FOR CHAPTER 10

Albert and Hahnel, *Unorthodox Marxism*, (Boston: South End Press, 1978).

Albert and Hahnel, *Marxism and Socialist Theory*, (Boston: South End Press, 1981).

Albert and Hahnel, Looking Forward: Participatory Economics for the Twenty First Century, (Boston: South End Press, 1991a).

Albert and Hahnel, *The Political Economy of Participatory Economics*, (Princeton: Princeton University Press, 1991b).

Albert and Hahnel, "Socialism As It Was Always Meant To Be," (*Review of Radical Political Economics*, Vol. 24; No. 3 & 4, 1992a).

Albert and Hahnel, "Participatory Planning," (*Science and Society* Spring 1992b).

Bardhan and Roemer, "'Market Socialism': A Case for Rejuvenation," (*Journal of Economic Perspectives*, Summer 1992).

Bowles, Sam, "What Markets Can and Cannot Do," (*Challenge*, July/August 1991).

Breitenbach, Burden, and Coates, *Features of a Viable Socialism*, (Hemel Hempstead: Harvester Wheatsheaf, 1990).

Brus and Laski, *From Marx to the Market*, (Oxford: Clarendon Press, 1989).

Devine, Pat, *Democracy and Economic Planning*, (Boulder: Westview Press, 1988).

Devine, Pat, "Market Socialism or Participatory Planning?" (*Review of Radical Political Economics*, Vol. 24; No. 3 & 4, 1992).

Ellerman, David, *The Democratic Worker-Owned Firm*, (Winchester Mass: Unwin Hyman, 1990).

Folbre, Nancy, Contribution to "A Roundtable on Participatory Economics," Z *Magazine*, July/August, 1991.

Hagar, Mark, Contribution to "A Roundtable on Participatory Economics," *Z Magazine*, July/August, 1991.

Hahnel and Albert, *Quiet Revolution in Welfare Economics*, (Princeton, NJ: Princeton University Press, 1990).

Hahnel, Robin, "Cooperacion International Si, NAFTA, No!" (*Z Magazine*, April 1993).

Harrington, Michael, *Socialism, Past and Future*, (Boston: Little Brown, 1989).

E.K. Hunt and R.C. D'Arge, "On Lemmings and Other Acquisitive Animals: Propositions on Consumption," *(Journal of Economic Issues*, June 1973).

Le Grand and Estrin, eds., "Market Socialism", (Oxford: Clarendon Press, 1989).

Mandel, William M, "Socialism: Feasibility and Reality" in *Science and Society*, Vol. 57, No. 3, Fall 1993

Miller, David, Market, State and Community: Theoretical Foundations of "Market Socialism", (Oxford: Clarendon Press, 1989).

Nove, Alec, *The Economics of Feasible Socialism Revisited*, (London: Harper-Collins Academic, 1991).

Schweickart, David, "Socialism, Democracy, Market, and Planning: Putting the Pieces Together," (*Review of Radical Political Economics*, Vol. 24; No. 3 & 4, 1992).

Schweickart, David, *Against Capitalism*, (Cambridge: Cambridge University Press, 1993).

Tilly, Chris, "Dilemmas for Socialists," *Dollars and Sense*, July/August, 1992.

Weisskopf, Thomas, "Toward a Socialism for the Future in the Wake of the Demise of the Socialism of the Past," (*Review of Radical Political Economics*, Vol. 24; No. 3 & 4, 1992).

Afterword

What's next for parecon?

"To create a new culture does not only mean to make original discoveries on an individual basis. It also and especially means to critically popularize already discovered truths, make them, so to speak, social, therefore give them the consistency of basis for vital actions, make them coordinating elements of intellectual and social relevance."

—Antonio Gramsci

"The Lord of the Flies hung in space before him.

'What are you doing out here all alone? Aren't you afraid of me?'

Simon shook.

'There isn't anyone to help you. Only me. And I'm the beast.'

Simon's mouth labored, brought forth audible words.

'Pig's head on a stick.'"

—William Golding

IN 1991 ROBIN HAHNEL AND I PUBLISHED two books presenting the participatory economic model in considerable detail. In the ensuing months and years there has been much related discussion and debate, some of which is summarized in chapter 10 of this book. At this point, it seems that moving from unorganized discussion to a more organized political process makes sense.

What can be done? As a start:

• The participatory economic vision can be criticized, corrected, improved, refined, popularized (via courses, articles, talks, etc.) and disseminated.

• Elements of the vision can be incorporated into the daily work relations of existing organizations and projects, much as has been accomplished by South End Press and Arbeiter Ring Publishing, and as could be undertaken in other progressive projects and workplaces, dwelling places and communities.

• Efforts can be undertaken to develop and then act on strategic and programmatic agendas based in participatory economic vision but grounded in immediate possibilities.

• The relation of parecon to questions of kinship, gender, sex, culture, and political vision can be explored.

• People working on the economic vision and its application can provide support and aid to one another, by sharing information and examples.

How can all this occur?

The people inclined to participate in any of the above tasks are scattered across the world with few of them in any one place, at least for now. So if there is to be a structure that facilitates all these practices, it would have to be a very far flung one, indeed. Also, it would have to operate very inexpensively, there being no available budget.

Two related possibilities come to mind: reading or study groups and an umbrella Institute for Participatory Economics.

Reading groups are a spontaneous affair. A person decides to form one, gathers some friends or work mates, and the process of reading and discussing the material begins. The only way we can facilitate this is to provide much reduced rates for the needed books. So:

If you set up a reading group you can buy books in bulk, five or more copies at a time, for 50 percent off list price. Just send a letter indicating that you are going to have a reading group, the number of copies of this book that you need, and the fee, to Arbeiter Ring Publishing. (You can also write to South End Press, under the same terms, for copies of *Looking Forward*, a more extensive presentation of parecon. Their address is 116 St. Botolph Street, Boston, MA 02115-4818 USA.)

What about an institute? We don't have money for a residence. And it wouldn't be all that useful in any event, given the dispersed nature of the proposed organization's constituency. What we can do, however, is to put the proposed institute online.

Thus, on the telecommunications system Left On Line, we will establish the Institute for Participatory Economics. To belong to this one will have to be a member of Left On Line, seriously committed to developing participatory economics, and also specifically and self-consciously join the Institute, but at no extra charge. Business will be conducted privately by the members in online forums for discussing the vision and collectively pursuing all the other agendas noted earlier.

And on the public World Wide Web, we will echo the products of the Institute, though without the participatory component of people being able to partake of all the more in-depth discussions. On the Web, where folks may only be curious or critical, for interaction we will only have an introductory forum for talking broadly about the model and for answering questions about the Institute and how to join, should folks be interested.

So, reader, if you want to partake in the public Web option just aim your browser at *www.lbbs.org* and then follow the links to the Participatory Economics section. But if you want to join the institute, first you will need to join Left On Line. To learn more about that and to also join, if you so decide, aim your browser at *www.lol.shareworld.com* and then examine the visitors information offered there.

Colophon

Colophons—notes that explain the design, typesetting, and printing of a book—are becoming increasingly rare in modern publishing. We feel that all parts of the process of producing a book have political implications, and include these short paragraphs as a declaration of our pride in and responsibility for our work as designers, typesetters, and publishers. As well, a colophon can provide a rare view of the usually unseen, but often fascinating, world of book production.

Thinking Forward is set in Caslon, a contemporary version of the typeface first designed by William Caslon in 1722. We have chosen it because of its classic, open appearance, which makes it an elegant and readable typeface. These qualities are no doubt responsible for Caslon's enduring popularity; it has been in wide use since being adopted by English printers in the early eighteenth century, when it replaced the primarily Dutch typefaces that had long predominated. Caslon is most often criticised for its italics, which are considered unnecessarily florid.

The main text is set in 11-point type on a 120% line. The questions are set in Myriad, 10-point type on a 12-point line.

The book was printed and bound by Hignell Printing of Winnipeg, Manitoba on 50lb. #2 offset paper.

The images that precede each chapter were drawn with love by Tony Doyle. They were scanned electronically, then output along with the rest of the book, and sent to the printer camera-ready.

About Arbeiter Ring

ARBEITER RING is a not-for-profit, worker-owned and collectively-run publishing house. We strive to be an activist press, to publish contemporary and accessible writing that amplifies the voices and documents the struggle for social change.

One of the most effective tools for indoctrination into mainstream ideology is still the written word. For a mainstream, capitalist publishing house, interested primarily in the profitability of their titles, whether or not anyone ever actually reads their books is irrelevant. Think about that. By contrast, at Arbeiter Ring we see ourselves as an activist press. This means that our first principle when choosing which books to publish is their political impact.

We feel there is a way for the structure of Arbeiter Ring to reflect the humane and egalitarian ideals that are the impulse behind its creation. To that end, we have modelled our collective structure on the principles of participatory economics, a good introduction to which you are holding in your hands.

Arbeiter Ring ("Worker's Circle") is named after a turn-of-the-century union formed by radical Eastern European Jewish immigrants, which, by 1915, had nearly 50 000 members in branches across North America. In Winnipeg, the Arbeiter Ring served as an umbrella organization for progressive and radical groups in the community, operating on the social, cultural, and ideological level.